THE CRUCIFIX, THE FLAG, AND A BLACKBOARD

A Survey of Catholic Education in the United States
and Those Who Contributed to Its Success

The CRUCIFIX, the FLAG, and a BLACKBOARD

A Survey of Catholic Education in the United States
and Those Who Contributed to Its Success

Wayne Merckling

Leonine Publishers
Phoenix, Arizona

Copyright © 2015 Wayne Merckling

All rights reserved. No part of this book may be reproduced or transmitted in any form or by any means, electronic or mechanical, including photocopying, recording, or by any information storage or retrieval system now existing or to be invented, without written permission from the respective copyright holder(s), except for the inclusion of brief quotations in a review.

Published by Leonine Publishers LLC
Phoenix, Arizona
USA

ISBN-13: 978-1-942190-08-0

Library of Congress Control Number: 2014958928

Printed in the United States of America
10 9 8 7 6 5 4 3 2 1

Visit us online at www.leoninepublishers.com
For more information: info@leoninepublishers.com

Dedicated, with gratitude, to

The Marist Brothers, particularly those who served in Christ the King High School, Queens, New York, and St. Mary's High School, Manhasset, New York;

The Basilian Fathers of St. John Fisher College, Rochester, New York;

The Vincentian Fathers of St. John's University, Queens, New York;

The Sisters of Notre Dame de Namur who served Our Lady of the Miraculous Medal School in Ridgewood, Queens, New York;

And the lay educators who served in all.

CONTENTS

PREFACE xi
ACKNOWLEDGEMENTS xvii
INTRODUCTION 1

CHAPTER 1

THE FOUNDATIONS OF CATHOLIC EDUCATION

Greco-Roman Education 5
Early Christian Education and the First Monasteries . . 6
The Dark Ages. 8
The Middle Ages 9
The Moslems 10

CHAPTER 2

THE FIRST UNIVERSITIES AND THE REFORMATION

The Mendicant Orders 15
Birth of the Universities 17
The Reformation and the Church's Response 19
The Jesuits. 20
Teaching Congregations 23

CHAPTER 3

CATHOLIC EDUCATION IN COLONIAL AND REVOLUTIONARY AMERICA

Missionaries and the Early Years 29
Colonial Education 30
Colonial Colleges 33

CHAPTER 4

THE GROWTH OF AMERICAN CATHOLIC UNIVERSITIES

Expansion 35
Growth of American Colleges 35
The French Influence 37
Colleges Become Universities 42

CHAPTER 5

CATHOLIC EDUCATION IN THE NINETEENTH CENTURY

The Bishops 47
Early Problems for Catholic Education 49
Growth of Catholic High Schools 50

CHAPTER 6

BROTHERS, PRIESTS, AND CATHOLIC SECONDARY EDUCATION

Secondary Education 55
Vocational Education 59
The Role of Brothers in Education 61
High School Curriculum 63

CHAPTER 7

MOVING INTO THE THIRD MILLENNIUM

Reacting to Change 71
Trends in Higher Education 74

CHAPTER 8

THE TWENTY-FIRST CENTURY AND THE FUTURE

Institutes 79
. . . . 82

CHAPTER 9

SISTERS: PARTNERS IN AMERICAN EDUCATION

Background 87
Sisters Come to America 88
American Congregations 89
French Congregations 90
Immigration and Additional Congregations 93
Academies and Catholic Higher Education
   for Young Women 96
Teacher Training 98
The Twentieth Century 100

CHAPTER 10

JUST PASSING THROUGH

Education .105
Teaching 107
School Administration 108
The Catholic Lens 113

PREFACE

As the high school that I had served as principal for the past seven years started its second semester, I packed the last boxes in my office and prepared to speak to the students and staff at a general assembly for the last time. Could it have been more than forty years ago that I walked into a classroom for the first time as a high school math teacher? Two generations of students and hundreds of colleagues later, I completed a professional journey that included a number of different schools and positions. The last time I strolled down memory lane was when I completed my doctoral degree, fifteen years earlier.

It was raining heavily on that cold January day while we waited in double file for the procession to begin in Alumni Hall at St. John's University in Queens, New York. As I donned the red robe and glanced at the black stripes on my sleeve representing a doctoral degree, I realized that my life had come full circle. I grew up in Queens many years ago, and it was there during my high school days at Christ the King that I seriously realized that I wanted to be a teacher. So much has happened since then. It seems that I have lived many lifetimes as I think of the thousands of students who have passed through my classrooms and offices.

The thought of teaching five sections of geometry to forty or forty-five tenth-grade boys at a time seemed an interesting challenge. I spent the summer between my college graduation and my first day of teaching in preparation; Euclidean geometry was one of the few math courses not taught at the college level. My last and only experience in geometry was my own high school education. I was energized by the opportunity of teaching the same subject as my own geometry teacher, Mr. Joe Lang, whom I highly respected. When I was a student at Christ the King, he taught my class an entire geometry course in one semester and Algebra II the next. My first day as a teacher marked the beginning of a journey—one that was still in progress as I waited to be hooded by my own mentor.

It was a fitting time in my life to look back, reflect, and try to understand all that has happened during my career. It has been and remains a rewarding, challenging, and interesting journey—one that I hope will be taken by many younger, talented people, all hoping to make a difference in the lives of their students.

Countless men and women made a difference in my life and influenced my career. Some, like Joe Lang, were teachers and coaches, raising their own children while they worked with us. Many others were religious who had dedicated themselves totally to educating us in Catholic schools.

Today, following a period when Catholic schools closed in large numbers and the legions of religious men and women who labored in their classrooms have dissipated, those of us who benefited from their care and training should not allow the memory of their dedication to fade from history. If the large armies of us who try to quietly carry on their work allow their efforts to be forgotten, we are not validating what they have done and what we continue to do. Without their teaching, encouragement, philosophy, and guidance, we would not have dedicated our lives to education. And so, while curiosity about their work led me to begin the research for this book, the task evolved into a labor of love.

Throughout my career, the religious and lay teachers who taught me, and those with whom I had the privilege of working, remain as mentors in my heart. A parish priest taught me how to work with youth, and my own teachers in a parish elementary school and in a diocesan high school taught me how to teach and counsel students. My college chaplain taught me how to uphold Catholic values, and the professors who taught me gave me a deeper understanding of Catholicism; later in life, the brothers I worked with taught me how to be an administrator for an educational community. Those lessons are not forgotten.

In part, this book is devoted to all who taught me as they carried out the vision of their founders or the Vatican's teaching on the lay apostolate in the classroom. As I researched their work, I could not help but be more concerned about the impact of the declining number of religious in America and the continuing trend of Catholic school closings in many parts of our country. The thought occurred to me that children and young adults would no longer experience Catholic education as I had. Most would never have the privilege of being taught by a sister, brother, priest, or layperson in a Catholic Christian environment. My fear was that the legacy of these dedicated professionals and the founders of their orders would be forever lost. Though I was aware that Catholic school administrators emphasize the importance of the charisms of the founding orders of their schools to their faculty, I searched for what is available for others to learn about these lost traditions and the lessons that can be passed on from them. My conclusion was that there is literature available from each religious congregation concerning its charism and its contributions to education, along with a number of works concerning the activities of the female congregations. However, there does not seem to be a great deal of literature concerning the educational work of priests and brothers. Further, I did not discover a work that connected the efforts of all those who developed the Catholic educational tradition and placed it in the context of American education. Thus, the present book represents part of my attempt to share what I found with others.

I offer my work not as one of scholarship but rather as one of gratitude to all who made my Catholic education possible. In the process of researching the history of Catholic education, I discovered that the Internet contains a wealth of information published by religious orders, colleges, universities, and educational institutes. Thus, my sources are a blend of paper and electronic resources that I hope others can use to begin similar efforts. Although the electronic resources were retrieved over a twelve-year period, every one listed among the primary or secondary sources was validated during the winter of 2013–2014.

This book is my attempt to give others an opportunity to study the development of our Catholic educational heritage, to reexamine the legacy we have been given, and to remind all of the privilege of the work that we carry out. Its purpose is to trace the historical significance of Catholic education, to record the knowledge that it passes on, and, in particular, to honor all the men and women who made so many contributions to the formation of Catholic youth in America over the course of four centuries.

My research can be summarized by the following salient points: The knowledge that we share in Catholic schools and universities began to develop in pre-Christian times and was preserved, expanded, and passed on by a legion of religious and lay scholars. Many of the communities of religious who brought this legacy to our nation were founded in times of revolution, either political or religious. Many of the religious who arrived at our shores came at the invitation of bishops who afforded the leadership required to build our vast educational system of schools, colleges, seminaries, and universities. In addition to facing hardship and sometimes prejudice after they arrived, religious communities often had to be flexible in adjusting their charism (that is, the main focus of their ministry) in order to serve the people around them.

Because this flexibility is still found in their now-depleted congregations, most of these communities still exist and continue their work. Catholic schools and universities are able to continue their services because of the vast number of dedicated laymen and laywomen who oversee, administer, and teach in them. Finally, the fruit of their labor (as was true in centuries past) continues to be an army of practicing Catholics who live their faith in their professional lives.

On a more personal note, this book is a consideration of how the efforts of my own teachers, professors, and colleagues affect me both as an individual and as a professional. I hope to share this with both practicing and future teachers so that they will have a better understanding of the importance of the work that they do. It is my belief that if we take the time to study the founders who dedicated their lives to Catholic education and to appreciate the challenges that they faced, we can adopt them as mentors of a sort. Let us hope that their success in overcoming their own obstacles and personal limitations will encourage and assist us as we face ours, so that we may successfully continue the work that was undertaken by their spiritual sons and daughters.

ACKNOWLEDGEMENTS

I thank Michael Sheerin, F.M.S., for his quotation about life as a Marist Brother and information about St. Marcellin Champagnat. Thanks also to Brother Donald Kelly, F.M.S., whom I have known since my high school days, for assisting me at the beginning of my teaching career and providing me with updated information about the Marist Brothers. I would also like to acknowledge the assistance of Dr. Patricia Bartle, formerly of the Office of the Diocese of Paterson, as well as my former colleagues Dr. Steven Racine and Dr. Matthew Scanlon.

Last but not least, thanks to my wife Susan, for her patience with me during this very long process.

INTRODUCTION

Our intellectual and educational culture is built upon a knowledge base that was initiated thousands of years before Christianity. It continued to develop under the Greeks, Romans, and early Christians, and it was recorded by monks in monasteries throughout the first millennium. Despite the challenges faced by the early Church and the decline of culture during the Dark Ages, our Catholic heritage continued to evolve. The first part of the Litany of the Saints invokes the names of our early leaders and martyrs through those difficult times. In a similar way, the work of Francis, Benedict, and Dominic did not end during the Reformation, when the Church was criticized for its mistakes. And today, the labors of John Baptist de La Salle, John Bosco, and countless others will not be terminated because of the events that occurred at the end of the twentieth century and that are occurring in the beginning of the twenty-first century. Their congregations came to America at the invitation of bishops; they traveled by ship and then made their way to their new homes. Some remained in the cities of their entry, while others traveled inland or even to the frontier lands. These brothers, priests, and sisters opened schools, orphanages, and hospitals. They dedicated themselves to their fellow immigrants, Native Americans, and all those who traveled west and explored new territories in search of a new life. These men and women brought the spirit of their founders with them. Many of the priests came as missionaries to the New World, seeking to introduce Catholicism to its inhabitants.

Although united in creed, they differed in many ways. Many of the teaching orders were created or revitalized after their leaders experienced the prejudice of anti-Catholicism in countries like Ireland, Germany, France, and England. Their countrymen fled to America in order to escape religious persecution. Many of the orders of brothers followed later to teach our nation's youth in high schools and universities across the country.

Regardless of how they began or what brought their founders here, the schools that these sisters, priests, and brothers established still reflect what was special to their orders. Their vows differed: some took the traditional vows of chastity, poverty, and obedience, and others added allegiance to a particular house or to a particular ministry, such as education.

Whatever the particulars of their congregation, the challenges that these religious faced in America were immense. Throughout the nineteenth century, many had to contend with growing urban populations, disease, poverty, anti-Catholicism, or the fear of being attacked by Native Americans while they moved westward. Most religious communities, regardless of their original charism, began by trying to serve the needs of those around them. As with many others, what they envisioned and what God called them to do often differed. Some of the congregations began by serving the poor and ended up teaching the wealthy, the powerful, and the privileged. Some orders originally devoted to a quiet life of devotion were called to a life of Christian faith in action— in classrooms, hospitals, orphanages, and so forth. What was common to all of these communities was that they did not stubbornly adhere to the limits of their original intentions; rather, they listened to their call and served the needs presented to them.

Many religious teachers were beckoned by frontier bishops to serve their cities and their growing populations.

These bishops had to build political and business ties to get what they needed for the people in their dioceses. Hundreds of schools could not have been built and staffed without a lot of networking on their part.

As the various religious orders established themselves in this country, they garnered vocations from their colleagues and those they taught. Their congregations increased in membership as the school systems grew. Some congregations wrote their own books, and they all followed the pedagogy they were trained in by their superiors. These religious were careful to nurture the mission and philosophy of their founders. As the years turned to decades and centuries, each religious community renewed and updated its mission and aligned it with the needs of the peoples they served.

The number of religious educators peaked in the 1960s, just as the enrollment in their schools did. After Vatican II, US Church membership was impacted by suburban growth, urban flight, and the social and political upheaval of the time. The membership of all the religious congregations decreased, new vocations fell dramatically, and their schools closed, combined, or relocated. Those that remain open are left to the care of the laity and the few remaining religious. What follows is the story of the dedicated men and women who started it all.

CHAPTER 1

THE FOUNDATIONS OF CATHOLIC EDUCATION

Greco-Roman Education

Students of world history know that the ancient civilizations of Egypt and Babylonia made early advances in discovering what they considered truths about astronomy and navigation. These civilizations had their own written language, and their artists left us records of their work—records found on buildings, monuments, and sculptures discovered centuries later. Historians note that the Turanian or Mongol tribes of the valley of the Euphrates were probably the first to establish schools. Later, classical Roman, Greek, and Hebrew civilizations expanded, edited, and refined the knowledge base left by these ancient civilizations.

We teach our students that Greek education emphasized physical education, philosophy, and mathematics, while the Romans were more interested in using education in law to prepare students to be good citizens. If one looks at these ideals collectively, they should seem somewhat familiar—that is, they resemble some of the intended outcomes of American Catholic education, which also has religious, cultural, and political components. Who would disagree with the notion that Catholic schools should be graduating knowledgeable

Christians who understand the sacramentality of their lives, who are educated so as to be informed citizens, and who value the culture passed on to them? Christians took the secular knowledge of all these cultures and blended it with their religious beliefs. This process developed throughout the first century AD, and in some ways it is still occurring. Each civilization had to decide whether the spiritual or metaphysical was more important than the scientific, or what early Christians called the "profane." Christians, like the Hindus, eventually contributed to the development of mathematics, science, and other disciplines; however, the spiritual realm remained the most important.

Thomas Storck writes that the early Christian missionaries brought to northern and central Europe "all the intellectual heritage of the Hebrews, Greeks, and Romans. Latin Christian civilization became extended through Europe, and together with the lands of Greek culture, resulted in Christian Western civilization."[1]

Early Christian Education and the First Monasteries

Early Christian education was concerned with preparing students for baptism; these students were called catechumens. The teachers were members of the congregation who taught according to the example of the Apostles. The students were children, converts, or clergy and were required to have different degrees of knowledge of the books of the Bible and of the accepted doctrines and practices of the early Church. As time passed, the clergy eventually took over the catechumens' schools. Rena Foy, in the book *The World of Education*, points out that

> By combining with the original teachings of Christ, certain elements from the ceremonies and rites of Hebrew morality, concepts from

Greco-Roman philosophy . . . and ceremonies from some of the popular religions of the eastern world, Christianity was gradually adapted to the temperaments and customs of the diverse peoples to whom its message was carried.[2]

"In this formative period, Christian education was dedicated to the training of children, converts, and clergy in the doctrines and practices of the early Church."[3] During the succeeding centuries, the Church produced leaders who did not always agree on what type of education was appropriate. "Some of the greatest theologians and fathers like St. Basil, St. Gregory Nazianzen, and St. Gregory of Nyssa studied the classics under pagan masters and were therefore in favor of sending Christian youths to non-Christian schools on the grounds that literary studies would enable them to better defend their faith. St. Basil believed that the classics had a place in Christian education, while others like John Chrysostom, Ambrose, Jerome, and Augustine, did not agree."[4]

As the years progressed, the monasteries that would later become important for education and the transmission of knowledge began to open. These were not new to religion; they already existed in the Far East. Scholars seem to agree that Anthony of Egypt initiated Christian monasticism. During the fourth century, monasteries spread to many locations, including Bethlehem, Jerusalem, Constantinople, and Rome.

Monastery schools not only provided training for members of the religious orders but also educated children in a more general curriculum. In addition to offering education, the monasteries were the only libraries, research centers, and publishing houses of this time period. "We owe much to the Christian monasteries for preserving and spreading learning and culture. They not only preserved ancient knowledge but brought forth chronicles and religious writers of their own, as well as sacred writing by the Early Church."[5]

By the fifth century, famous theologians—including such names as St. Basil, St. Gregory, and St. Jerome—had formalized the content that is still taught in churches and schools today. In Bethlehem, St. Jerome founded a school for boys that was open to those who were not studying to be religious, and St. Benedict founded monasteries that had schools associated with them. Speaking of St. Benedict, St. John Baptist de La Salle, a more modern famous educator, states, "The education of children was regarded of such great importance by this saint that he educated and cared for a great number of them in his monasteries. He took care to have them instructed in learning and in piety."[6] Historians acknowledge that during these years the Benedictines were the chief religious, civilizing, and educating influence in the Western Church. In fact, the Western monastic tradition of the Middle Ages—which was founded principally on the *Life of St. Benedict* in the *Dialogues* and the *Rule of St. Benedict*—was deeply Benedictine in character.

The Dark Ages

The period now called the Dark Ages was a time during which Europe was attacked and most traces of classical civilization disappeared. Fortunately, the monasteries of Ireland provided a base from which monks continued Christian work. Scholars traveled to these monasteries to continue their work.

"Saint Patrick founded Armagh where he built his church, monastery, and school. Through the work and fame of the great schools which were to develop there, it was to become not only the ecclesiastical capital of Ireland but the capital of civilization."[7] Saint Columba extended the work of opening monasteries to Scotland. English scholars traveled to

Ireland's schools. In addition to the monastery schools, other schools were opened by teachers who had notable reputations.

THE MIDDLE AGES

Historians point to the reign of King Charles the Great (742–814), more commonly known as Charlemagne, as the beginning of the end of the Dark Ages. He was known for encouraging religious to open schools in villages, and his palace school became famous because of the improvements he made. Charlemagne gathered the most noteworthy European scholars, including Alcuin of York, who directed the palace school. "In addition to stimulating the Church to establish village schools and to improve monastic education, Charlemagne enlarged and improved the palace school for the benefit of his family and nobility, adults as well as children."[8]

During this period, a handwriting script was developed and used by monks for copying manuscripts. Scholars point to this development as crucial to building the literacy of Western Civilization. King Alfred, also noted for his interest in scholarship, continued to improve monastic schools.

As one reads about the development of education, it becomes clear that in some locations, such as the diocese of Soissons, before the end of the ninth century both boys and girls attended schools attached to parish churches. The laity had access to parochial schools that taught religion in addition to the seven liberal arts. Since there were few textbooks, the method of teaching was lecture, and the students would record the texts and the teacher's comments. There were many noted educators in the first eight centuries of the Christian era, including "St. Isidore of Seville who is sometimes called 'The Schoolmaster of the Middle Ages'. His books and schools helped shape the education, the culture of medieval Europe, and so, of western civilization."[9]

Some other well-known individuals made their own contributions. Saint Boniface established a school in every monastery he founded in Germany, and St. Augustine and his monks set up schools wherever they went. Some monasteries were known for their particular skill in certain branches of knowledge. For example, lectures in medicine were given by monks at St. Benignus in Dijon, the monastery of St. Gall had a school of painting and engraving, and lectures in Greek, Hebrew, and Arabic could be heard at certain German monasteries.

Eventually, local councils and Church synods called for the opening of schools. It was a challenging period because invading barbarians destroyed monasteries, and then the monks had to rebuild them. "As time went on, cathedral schools were opened by bishops, which taught secular subjects in addition to theology, subjects from classical antiquity and professional preparation for medicine, law, and teaching. From 1000–1300 some of the cathedral schools evolved into universities."[10]

The Moslems

One of the developments that had a major impact on what knowledge was handed down to future generations of educators was the Moslem invasion of Western Europe in the eighth century. A century earlier, the Moslems conquered Alexandria, thus gaining access to a wealth of knowledge that had developed up until that time. As a result, Arab Moslems soon devoted much time to the study of the mathematics, science, and philosophy that the Greeks had developed.

As the conquering Moslems moved through Europe into Spain, they took the work of Greek scholarship with them. "Their Arabian culture was a synthesis of Mohammedan religion, Arabian language, Persian architecture and science and

Greek philosophy. The civilization that the Arabs planted in Spain continued into the Middle Ages and had considerable influence on university life and philosophical studies in Christian Europe."[11]

"Arabic civilization was at its height in the East in the 9th and 10th centuries and in Spain during the 11th and 12th. The transmission function of Arabic culture in history, geography, science and math was always important. The translation of Arabic works into Latin in the latter Middle Ages and the huge repute enjoyed by Arab thinkers in Europe testify to the quality of the culture."[12]

Endnotes

1. Thomas Storck. "What Is Western Culture?" From www.ewtn.com/library/THEOLOGY/FR94102.htm.

2. Rena Foy (1968). *The World of Education*. New York: Collier Macmillan Ltd., pp. 30–31.

3. Wilds and Lottich (1961). *The Foundations of Modern Education*. New York: Holt, Rinehart, and Winston, p. 112.

4. *The Catholic Encyclopedia*, copyright 1913 by Robert Appleton Co. Online edition, copyright 1999 by Kevin Knight. www.newadvent.org/cathen/05295b.htm. Entry: Education.

5. Wilds and Lottich (1961). *The Foundations of Modern Education*. New York: Holt, Rinehart, and Winston, p. 120.

6. John Baptist de La Salle, translated by Richard Arnandez and Augustine Loes, edited by Augustine Loes and Francis Huether (1994). *Meditations*. 1994 Christian Brothers' Conference, Maryland, p. 205.

7. Seumas MacManus (1921). *The Story of the Irish Race*. Old Saybrook, CT: Konecky & Konecky, p. 118.

8. Frederick Binder (1970). *Education in Western Civilization: Selected Readings*. Toronto, Ontario: Macmillan Co., p. 86.

9. Bert Ghezzi (2000). *Voices of the Saints*. New York: Doubleday, p. 324.

10. Bill Cahoy (2003). "The Catholic Intellectual Tradition." From www.csbsju.edu/about/catholic-benedictine-tradition/catholic-identity/catholic-values/bill-cahoy-fall-forum.

11. W. Eugene Shields (1941). *History of Europe*. Fort Collins, CO: Roman Catholic Books, pp. 94–95.

12. J. M. Roberts (1993). *History of the World*. New York: Oxford University Press, pp. 269–270.

Additional Sources

Luella Cole (1965). *A History of Education: Socrates to Montessori*. New York: Holt, Rinehart, and Winston.

Mark C. Henrie (2000). *Students Guide to the Core Curriculum*. Wilmington, DE: ISI Books.

Robert Guisepi (1992). "Middle Ages: The Intellectual Synthesis of the High Middle Ages." From http://history-world.org/a_history_of_the_catholic_church.htm.

Thomas Flynn (2003). "Athens and Jerusalem, Paris and Rome," in *Faith and the Life of the Intellect*, edited by Hancock and Sweetman, Washington, DC: Catholic University of America Press.

Thomas Storck. "What is Western Culture?," in *Faith and Reason*, Spring 1994. Front Royal, VA: Christendom Press. From www.ewtn.com/library/theology/FR94102.htm.

Jean Leclercq (1982). *The Love of Learning and the Desire for God: A Study of Monastic Culture*. New York: Fordham University Press.

The Catholic Encyclopedia, copyright 1913 by Robert Appleton Co. Online edition, copyright 1999 by Kevin Knight. Entries:
  Religious Life. www.newadvent.org/cathen/12748b.htm.
  Carolingian Schools. www.newadvent.org/cathen/03349c.htm.
  Schools. www.newadvent/cathen/13554b.htm.

J. L. Spalding (1901). "Religion, Agnosticism and Education." Address to NEA. From https://www3.nd.edu/Departments/Maritain/etext/raae.htm.

CHAPTER 2

THE FIRST UNIVERSITIES AND THE REFORMATION

From roughly 600–1000, monastic schools were the principal centers of education and learning. Since reading and study were part of monastic culture, monasteries created libraries by copying books, not just religious ones. Later in the period, cathedral schools became common and included instruction in religious and secular subjects including preparation for the professions such as medicine, law and education. From 1000–1300 some of these cathedral schools evolved into universities in part staffed by several religious congregations.[1]

The Mendicant Orders

The beginning of the thirteenth century saw the birth of a new type of religious order whose members lived their lives outside of the monastery. They were called mendicant orders, meaning they relied on alms since their members did not live in a specific monastery. The mendicant orders were as important to the High Middle Ages as the original monastic orders had been during earlier times. Four orders of this type became famous. Ironically—considering the major role they would eventually play in Catholic education—none of the four were originally founded for the purpose of teaching.

The Carmelites, founded in Palestine, eventually took up a mendicant lifestyle under the leadership of St. Simon Stock during the thirteenth century. Noted for their life of contemplation, the members of this order eventually served as teachers and missionaries. "St. Simon strove especially to implant the order at universities partly to secure for the religious the advantages of higher education and partly to increase the number of vocations."[2]

Another famous mendicant order was the one initiated by St. Francis of Assisi. One thing that makes this famous individual special is that St. Francis was never ordained a priest. He founded the Franciscan First Order, which developed into the Friars Minor, in 1209. "While monks like St. Benedict and Bernard had been intent upon withdrawal from the world, St. Francis felt that approach was incompatible with his new mission of bringing holiness into the market place. His brethren were not to retire behind monastery walls . . . but to go out into the world . . . as Christ's ambassadors. . . . The Franciscan movement certainly inaugurated a new era in the history of religious orders."[3]

Although they were not originally involved in scholarly work, under the influence of St. Bonaventure (1221–1274) and the leadership of St. Bernadine of Siena (1380–1444), the Franciscans gradually incorporated scholarship into their tradition. Learning became part of Franciscan life, and later St. Bernadine required his men to study theology and canon law. The friars began to attract European scholars and theologians, with the result that they became an important force in the universities of their day.

The Dominicans, named after their founder St. Dominic, began in 1216 as preachers and defenders of the Church, and they still regard these two activities as the core of their ministry. They established small houses of preachers in locations such as Paris and Bologna. "Since the first duty of the preachers was to expound Christian truth, the task required educated men and therefore Dominic declared study a duty. . . . Dominic was the first founder of an order to make study the principal occupation of its members and to give it an importance equal to that of prayer."[4]

St. Dominic's desire to encourage scholarship led him to establish foundations in the university cities of Europe. His was the first religious order to be represented in the faculty of the University of Paris; it possessed two chairs there. Dominicans also founded residences of higher studies in many of Europe's cultural centers. Their schools taught a comprehensive curriculum and were open to all. As St. Dominic's spiritual sons developed respect as educators, older orders employed Dominicans to preside over their theological schools, and popes chose them for Roman schools.

The fourth mendicant order of the period was the Augustinians, initiated in 1244. They followed the Rule of St. Augustine, which he wrote for his monastery around the beginning of the fifth century. Like their namesake, who authored a number of works and valued scholarship, the Augustinians promoted education for their members, and eventually they were associated with many of the major universities in Europe.

Birth of the Universities

Thus, the mendicant orders, though not intended by their founders to be teaching orders, were flexible enough to embrace the concept of education and eventually supplied the majority of the professors and students of the period. The universities at Paris and Bologna began as cathedral schools, while both Oxford and Cambridge began as an informal gathering of masters and students. These four institutions began to take form during the latter half of the twelfth century. This concept grew so quickly that by the time of the Reformation, eighty-one universities had been established.

The Dominicans settled in Paris in 1217 and in Oxford in 1221. The Franciscans began their university work in Paris in 1230 and in Oxford in 1224. The Carmelites and Augustinians had their own residences at both universities.

The curriculum for the bachelor of arts program in the medieval university was the trivium; only those in the master of arts program were trained in the quadrivium. Much of the vocabulary we associate with schools and education developed during this time, in addition to the academic calendar, what material was taught, and how it was taught.

At the time, it was important for universities to be recognized by the pope so that their teachings and degrees would be recognized throughout Europe. In the latter half of the thirteenth century, theology students began to be introduced to other disciplines, including the natural sciences, politics, and economics. Albert the Great (1206–1280) took advantage of discussions of these subjects, made possible by the scholarly work of the Arabs, and passed this knowledge along to his student Thomas Aquinas, who in turn used these subjects, as well as Aristotle's principles, to harmonize the Church's teachings with all of the available knowledge of the time. Aquinas's contributions to scholasticism, presented in his *Summa Theologica*, are still taught today. The scholastic arguments used by Aquinas developed from commentaries on ancient works and began to include questions developed by the professors who taught using the commentaries. The questions were supposed to be resolved through logical argument.

"Aquinas worried about students being bored when they were given lectures about questions that were not pertinent to their lives. He was also concerned about the practice of using books that had a structure that does not correspond to the way their minds worked. Finally, he believed that repetition led to boredom. Thomas respected the peoples' capacity to think for themselves."[5] Do the concerns that Thomas Aquinas raised over seven hundred years ago sound familiar?

"The Catholic tradition prides itself in its respect for learning and the intellectual life. The monastic scholars keeping the light of western civilization burning throughout the Dark ages, the cathedral schools, great universities of the middle ages, all witness to the Catholic conviction that faith and reason are colleagues, not adversaries, and that Athens has much to do with Jerusalem in the God-given task of faith seeking understanding."[6]

The Reformation and the Church's Response

Up to this point in history, Church and government worked together to build a network of universities. That practice ended when the Renaissance, originating in Italy, spread north. The message of this important period of history was that knowledge and learning were not for only the privileged but rather for all people. When the printing press made printed material readily available to all, this message became a reality.

Once common people started to read the Bible, they began to question what they had been taught about its contents. They were now reading the Bible without the benefit of the Church's teaching regarding Scripture and Tradition as two complementary and necessary sources of divine revelation. These changes, along with other Church-related issues, resulted in the Protestant Reformation, which in turn led to the secularization of schools. The Church manifested a new emphasis on Catholic education by encouraging the founding of teaching orders and congregations, reorganizing parish schools, and establishing new institutions for the training of Catholic children. In addition, theological seminaries were developed for the training of priests.

There are times when history seems to repeat itself. Just as anti-Christian sentiments in the first centuries after Christ contributed to the development of religious communities and monasteries, the Reformation led to the founding of teaching orders. Hundreds of years later, the French Revolution, which was anti-Catholic in philosophy, would lead to a surge of religious life in France, and anti-Catholic sentiments in America would lead to the development of one of the largest systems of Catholic schools in the world. These are examples of a trend that has influenced the development of the Church through the centuries: that is, members of the Church recognize and respond to needs when they arise.

The Jesuits

One group of men who answered the call to defend the Church during this turbulent period was led by Ignatius Loyola and was known as the Society of Jesus, or simply the Jesuits. "An essential characteristic of the Jesuit order is its complete departure from old monasticism. The change was determined by the needs of the time. The Jesuit's vocation is constant action in the service of the Church rather than contemplation. The Society of Jesus is characterized by intelligence placed at the service of religion."[7] Although Ignatius, like Francis and Dominic before him, did not envision education as his followers' charism, in 1547 the Jesuits were asked to educate young men in Sicily. They were so successful that other bishops began asking them to form schools in their dioceses. In a period of less than ten years, they had created thirty-five colleges (now called secondary schools) across Europe.

Jesuit schools established during the Counter-Reformation did not differ much from Protestant schools except in regard to religious instruction. Scholars describe the Society of Jesus as the first teaching order in the Catholic Church, insofar as the Jesuits were the first to undertake the founding, management, and staffing of schools as a formal ministry. (Recall that the Dominicans were for the most part still preachers, not teachers.)

As the Jesuit schools multiplied, it became clear that they would be easier to oversee if their teaching methods, curricula, and administrative procedures were consistent. The outcome was a Jesuit system of administration and teaching that developed over many years. This plan of studies was called the *Ratio Studiorum*; it was a set of definitive rules for teachers, school officials, and pupils. The Jesuits also developed the most diverse curricula for secondary and higher education compared to those of all the other teaching orders. The course of study at their lower colleges corresponded to that of the German gymnasium and included Latin. In the higher Jesuit colleges, the faculty of philosophy included scholastic philosophy along with Latin classics, logic, and rhetoric. In addition to the curriculum, the personal bond between teacher and pupil was regarded as important. As we will see in later chapters, the personal relationship between student and teacher was an important part of the educational experience in most Catholic schools.

In the Jesuit system, there was a lot of individual tutoring by the teacher as other students worked. Teaching was carried out through group instruction, but remedial education was individualized. Their schools were free, though they were not meant primarily for the poor. The Jesuits' contribution to schools includes division of work into grade levels, training of teachers in special colleges, practice teaching with supervision, and, most importantly, their attitude toward teaching as a calling. Although some of these ideas may not have been original, the Jesuits made them well known because of their many colleges. These very concepts remain in practice today.

The *Spiritual Exercises*, written by Ignatius Loyola as a form of religious experience later called a retreat, provided educators with both a goal and a methodology. It was the *Exercises* that first gave the Jesuit schools their cohesion and that formed the vision according to which the Jesuit teachers led their students to truth. Claudio Acquaviva compiled all of these ideas and published the *Ratio Studiorum* in 1599. The modernized version is still in use today.

In the Middle Ages, the Augustinians had a document known by the same name, and other orders had similar documents that were intended for training members of the order. The Jesuit *Ratio* was different because it was meant for the education of lay students as well as of religious and because it contained a plan of studies that included literature, history, and drama in addition to philosophy and theology. It was seen as a coherent and lucid statement of ideals, methods, and objectives shared not only by Jesuits but by all educators in early modern Europe. "Jesuit schools were unique in combining the model of the medieval university where students prepared for professions, and the model of the Renaissance humanistic academy which had a curriculum based on Greek and Latin, poetry, drama, oratory and history."[7] This new educational model was consistent with the original Christian legacy as well as with the philosophical approach developed by Thomas Aquinas.

There is no such thing as a Jesuit theory of a university, but there are principles in Ignatian spirituality and Jesuit practice that influence the Jesuits' approach to higher education. Ignatius modeled his vision of the educational institution on the Collegio Romano, now called the Gregorian University. Not all who were educated in that tradition have favorable memories. Father Hesburgh, former president of Notre Dame University, comments on this educational practice as follows: "My education at the Gregorian, I have to confess, left a lot to be desired. The teaching was rigid and unimaginative and almost rote; the syllabus and instruction methods had not changed, I think, from the way things were done when they started the University in 1558. Each major subject was boiled down to fifteen propositions, and at the end of each course you had to defend any one of those fifteen theses. . . . And yet, as rigid and old fashioned as the Gregorian was, it provided me with good intellectual discipline and a wonderful grounding in classical scholastic philosophy and theology."[8]

The Jesuits were not the only ones who answered the Church's call to provide education. A sixteenth-century religious group called the Order of Poor Clerics Regular of the Mother of God of Pious Schools founded by St. Joseph Calasanctius initiated a new form of religious life dedicated to education.

Teaching Congregations

Since the congregations of brothers who accepted the challenge of secondary education had such a positive impact on American education, it is important to understand their history and contributions. Some believe that the origins of religious brothers lie with St. Anthony of Egypt, who established a rule in the year 305. It should be noted that the term monk—from the Greek *monakhos*, indicating one who lives alone—came into use in the fourth century. Throughout the fourth century, monks founded monasteries in Egypt, Palestine, Turkey, Syria, and Greece. Saint Basil (329–379) is known as the father of Eastern monasticism. He was followed by Saints Gregory, Basil, and Martin of Tours, who established monasteries in the late fourth century. As discussed above, St. Benedict is known as the father of Western monasticism.

Another school of thought holds that a group of lay brothers was first instituted by St. John Gualbert at Vallombrosa, about 1038. "There are references though, that unordained religious did manual work earlier that century. For instance, records indicate that most of the Benedictines who were not originally clerics performed manual labor. By the thirteenth century, brothers from older orders such as the Benedictines were gradually joined by more active clerical orders like Franciscans and Dominicans. These were congregations that evolved outside of monastic walls, and were involved with reclaiming the Church following the Reformation. The most famous of the time, the Jesuits, also contained brothers."[9]

The first order of teaching brothers was the Christian Brothers, founded during the closing decades of the seventeenth century. John Baptist de La Salle's order of brothers, not priests, was dedicated to the education of the poor. Whole-group instruction, use of French rather than Latin, and ability grouping (grouping students by reading level and intelligence) were the hallmarks of the education that he and his brothers fostered. John Baptist de La Salle developed the "simultaneous method of teaching in which students were placed in graded levels and given textbooks to follow the lesson of the teacher. He applied this to all disciplines and later extended the concept to teaching older students."[10]

The brothers were directed to be attentive to each of their students and especially to those most in need. Unlike the Jesuits and later the Salesians, who incorporated physical recreation into their programs, the de La Salle Christian Brothers stressed silence, not activity. However, the Christian Brothers, like the Jesuits, quickly built a network of schools throughout France that taught religion as well as all other subjects suitable to the age group of the students. Since the vocation of teaching was central to their order, teacher-training programs, sometimes referred to as normal schools, were also developed. One would not guess by reading about de La Salle's accomplishments that there were many who fought him every step of the way. His own followers thought that the training he devised was too harsh, and outsiders did not share his belief regarding educating all rather than just the wealthy.

Nevertheless, de La Salle's legacy is so valued that hundreds of years later the Irish Christian Brothers of Edmund Rice, the Brothers of Mary of Marcellin Champagnat, and various congregations of teaching sisters referenced de La Salle's writings and traditions in establishing their own educational traditions.

In summary, some of the outstanding contributions of these Catholic orders were emphasis on a better type of professional training, respect for classical knowledge in addition to theology, and attention to the importance of how to teach and organize schools. Though the Jesuits developed graduate schools of law and medicine as well as of theology, many believe that it was in the field of teacher training that they, along with the de La Salle Christian Brothers, rendered their greatest service to education.

Endnotes

1. Bill Cahoy (2003). "The Catholic Intellectual Tradition." From www.csbsju.edu/about/catholic-benedictine-tradition/catholic-identity/catholic-values/bill-cahoy-fall-forum.

2. "The Carmelite Order." From www.newadvent.org/cathen/03354a.htm.

3. Walter Nigg (1959). *Warriors of God*. New York: Alfred A. Knopf, p. 220.

4. Ibid., p. 257.

5. www.villanova.edu/mission/spirituality/augustinians.htm.

6. Hancock and Sweetman, editors (2003). *Faith and Life of the Intellect*. Washington, DC: Catholic University of America Press, p. 2.

7. Boston College. "A Pocket Guide to Jesuit Education." From www.bc.edu/offices/mission/publications/guide/success.

8. Theodore M. Hesburgh with Jerry Reedy (1990). *God, Country, Notre Dame*. New York: Doubleday, p. 33.

9. Tim Unsworth. "Hope Remains for the Unheralded Brothers of God." *National Catholic Reporter*, February 22, 2002.

10. Gerard Rummery, FSC, (1987). "The Lasallian Teacher," title of his keynote address given at a Lasallian conference in Chicago, Illinois, November 19-22, 1987. From http://www.delasalle.org/convocation/resources-lassallian-spirtuality-articles/1.3.2.19a.html.

Other Sources

The Catholic Encyclopedia, copyright 1913 by Robert Appleton Co. Online edition, copyright 1999 by Kevin Knight. www.newadvent.org/cathen/. Entries:
Franciscan Friars
Universities

Dale Launderville (1997). "Love and Knowledge: The Heart of the Catholic Intellectual Tradition."

Glazier and Shelly, editors (1997). *Encyclopedia of American Catholic History*. Collegeville, MN: The Liturgical Press, pp. 164–167.

John McMann, editor (1990). *Oxford Illustrated History of Christianity*. Oxford University Press.

Tom O'Donogue (2012). *Catholic Teaching Brothers: Their Life in the English-Speaking World, 1891–1965*. New York: Palgrave Macmillan.

Electronic Sources

William Hinebusch. "The Dominican's Short History." From http://opcentral.org/blog/the-dominican's-short-history.htm.

John O'Malley. *Ratio Studiorum*, "Introduction." From http://www.bc.edu/sites/libraries/ratio/ratiointro.html.

Michael McMahon (2004). "The Jesuit Model of Education." Conference presentation. From www.edocere.org/articles/jesuit-model-education.htm.

"Dominicans of Adrian Trace History to Divine Preacher." From www.georgiabulletin.org/local/1964/05/21/c.

www.csbsju.edu

www.op.org

www.heritage.villanova.edu/augustine

www.maritain.nd.edu

www.newadvent.org/cathen/12345c.htm

www.cbu.edu/lasallian/overview.htm

"St. John Baptist de La Salle." From www.newadvent.org/cathen/08444a.htm.

www.cbc.lasallehist

www.cbu.edu/community/lasallehistory.html

CHAPTER 3

CATHOLIC EDUCATION IN COLONIAL AND REVOLUTIONARY AMERICA

Missionaries and the Early Years

Many of the early European missionaries entered the United States from our neighbors to the north and south. The Franciscans, Jesuits, and Dominicans came to the Americas with explorers from Western Europe. In the United States, most early information about the male orders was related to missionary work and priests' efforts in starting parishes; at times, brothers accompanied the priests. The first authenticated visit of priests to our shores occurred in 1521, when Ponce de León sailed from Puerto Rico to the gulf coast.

The Franciscans took up the work abandoned by the Jesuits, whose superior general had become dissatisfied with the results of their missions. By the middle of the seventeenth century, the Franciscans had introduced some twenty-six thousand Native Americans to Christianity. Many believe that Spanish Franciscans initiated Catholic education in the future colonies by opening a classical school in St. Augustine, Florida, in 1606. Meanwhile, in the North, Champlain was exploring the area between Canada and Vermont, and he brought the Recollect Fathers, a branch of the Franciscans, with him. In the West, French Jesuit priests migrated from Canada and began to educate Native Americans, including Kateri Tekakwitha. They had arrived in Wisconsin by 1661 and had settled along the Mississippi by 1673. Now, colleges in those northern areas such as Le Moyne and Marquette serve as reminders of their work.

"The records are incomplete but the first Catholic school in the colonies was established about 1640 at St. Mary's City, Md., by the Jesuits. The next clearly recorded foundation was in 1673 at Newton, Md., "[1]

The Franciscans, led by Friar Junípero Serra, initiated missions as they moved north through California. "The success of the mission schools . . . was due to a number of factors. Serra was able to gather around him a number of experienced, committed priests to staff each of his missions."[2] As the missions were growing in the West, the colonies were developing in the East. Since the missionaries were from Western Europe, American education developed from a base of European intellectual traditions and institutions. The first formal eastern schools appeared in the 1630s. The Boston Latin School, established in 1635, is usually considered the first town-supported school with a continuous history. "During the seventeenth century Catholic schools were also established in Florida and Louisiana by lay teachers who were joined by Franciscans, Jesuits, Capuchins, Carmelites, and Ursulines in the conduct of these schools."[3]

Colonial Education

America was the first modern Western nation founded by Protestants rather than Catholics. Thus, most of the schools of the colonies were Protestant. They taught the "four Rs" of religion, reading, writing, and arithmetic. The religion curriculum was taught with the Bible and the Psalter, along with the recently written New England Primer. Young people who learned a trade, especially those in the South, remained at home or served as apprentices.

Sunday schools, begun in the late eighteenth century, also provided a basic education for children of the working poor. On the secondary level, one school, the Latin grammar school, was the standard in all of the colonies. Here boys learned Latin and Greek in preparation for college. During colonial times, families who could afford it often sent their children abroad to attend colleges such as St. Omer's in Flanders or the European convent schools. To provide these young Americans with the proper preparation for this experience, the Jesuits opened schools such as those at Newton Manor and Bohemia Manor in Maryland. "Archbishop John Carroll was an example of a noted Catholic who benefited from this education before attending St. Omer's in France." The curriculum of the secondary schools of the time was classical, though there was no teacher training offered before the American Revolution.

Colonial Catholic schools that started out with the purpose of training future priests developed into a secondary and university system for men. These colleges added schools to transition adolescent boys from the halls of parish schools to the campuses founded by priests. It would not take long for orders of teaching brothers from France and Ireland to assist in this effort. They opened schools to help men to prepare for the university and to enter the world as informed and practicing Catholics. The priests who taught in the boys' schools were few in number and were often educated in Europe.

Maryland, in 1649, was the first colony to officially grant religious freedom. It should be noted that even before 1649, the first school in Baltimore, St. Patrick's, was a Catholic school. In addition, the Jesuits founded St. Mary's, the oldest Catholic church in the region, in 1640. Its college is now named Loyola University.

The curricula in Protestant and Catholic schools were similar. The goal of Protestant education was to develop a religious and moral life through one's own interpretation of the Bible, while Catholic education pursued religious and moral formation through the guidance of Catholic doctrine.

Maryland was not the only colony with a Catholic influence. Further north, the Jesuits taught Native American children such as Kateri Tekakwitha, who later became a teacher herself. They also opened the New York Latin School. Catholics in Maryland enjoyed religious freedom for a relatively short period of time because when a Protestant king ascended the English throne, Maryland became a royal colony and Catholics were no longer welcome there. The Latin School had to close.

Throughout the colonial period, education was provided in elementary and grammar schools and then in private academies. "The first academy was probably planned by Ben Franklin and opened in Philadelphia in 1753 and within a few decades became the prevailing type of secondary school for the American school system, rapidly replacing the Latin grammar school. They were open to both boys and girls and provided a broad curriculum including practical arts."[4]

At the end of the eighteenth century—after the American Revolution and during the period in which the American government was taking shape—the emphasis in schools shifted from providing religious education to developing good citizens and leaders for the new nation. Also during this time, Pope Pius VI appointed John Carroll as the first bishop of Baltimore, a diocese that included the whole of the settled colonies. In 1782, Catholics opened St. Mary's, considered the first Catholic school in the United States, in Philadelphia. Not long after, Carroll opened Georgetown as a boys' prep school. He also arranged for the Sulpicians, a French order noted for training priests, to build a seminary in Baltimore that was eventually named St. Mary's.

Colonial Colleges

As discussed earlier, Catholic universities have roots in Western culture that go back to the early thirteenth century. They, like the monasteries, served as educational and cultural centers and were staffed by various religious orders, including the Dominicans, Franciscans, and Benedictines. The same orders, with the addition of the Jesuits, brought the university concept to the Americas, including Mexico.

Endnotes

1. Lee Deighton, editor (1971). *Encyclopedia of Education, Vol. II.* Macmillan Company Free Press. Entry: Catholic Education in the United States, pp. 10-18.

2. Ibid., p. 10.

3. Thomas Hunt (2000). "History of Catholic Schools in the US: An Overview," in *Catholic School Leadership*, edited by Hunt, Oldenski, and Wallace. New York: Falmer Press, pp. 34–58.

4. Wilds and Lottich (1961). *The Foundations of Modern Education.* New York: Holt, Rinehart, and Winston, pp. 222–224.

Other Sources

Bayles and Hood (1966). *Growth of American Educational Thought and Practice.* New York: Harper and Rowe.

Harold Buetow (1985). *A History of United States Catholic Schooling.* Washington, DC: NCEA.

Glazier and Shelly, editors (1997). *Encyclopedia of American Catholic History*. Collegeville, MN: The Liturgical Press.

Hartzell Spence (1960). *The Story of America's Religions*. New York: Holt, Rinehart, and Winston.

Catherine Kealey and Robert Kealey (2003). *On Their Shoulders: A Short Biographical History of American Catholic Schools*. Washington, DC: NCEA.

Maria Mazzenga (2010). "The Cradle of Catholicism: Catholic Education in Baltimore," in *Urban Catholic Education*, edited by Hunt and Walch. Notre Dame, IN: Alliance for Catholic Education Press, pp. 9–26.

Electronic Sources

Evangelical Lutheran Church in America. From www.elca.org.

CHAPTER 4

THE GROWTH OF AMERICAN CATHOLIC UNIVERSITIES

Expansion

As our country's settlers moved west, a trail of colleges followed. Saint Louis University opened as a diocesan institution, closed in 1826, then reopened under the Jesuits three years later. As they spread throughout the country, Catholic colleges offered a more general education because each had a preparatory school associated with it. Naturally, they "prepped" their students for advancing to their own college. Eventually both male and female religious orders followed this custom, and some of these prep schools are still in existence today.

American bishops reorganized and encouraged the growth of colleges, but religious congregations founded and staffed most of them. By 1850, forty-two Catholic colleges, including Notre Dame, Fordham, and Villanova, had been founded.

Growth of American Colleges

American Catholic colleges tended to be founded in clusters, and these clusters were representative of the religious orders that served Catholic immigrants in different locations across America. The following sample will demonstrate how widespread these orders were.

After some individual missionaries of the order labored in the American wilderness, the Augustinians came from Ireland to Philadelphia in 1796, and they founded what became Villanova University about forty-five years later. They experienced continued growth in membership that allowed them to increase their involvement in both parish-based and secondary education.

The Benedictines significantly contributed to the expansion of educational institutions in the second half of the nineteenth century. Their communities of men were known for constructing a system of seminaries, high schools, and colleges. These schools were to some degree matched by the Benedictine sisters' educational institutions. The sons and daughters of St. Benedict were associated with German immigration. They opened a number of colleges, including Belmont College in North Carolina, St. Anselm's in New Hampshire, St. John's in Minnesota, and Benedictine University in Illinois. They were also involved in a system of high schools.

The Vincentians came to America in 1815 to staff a seminary in Louisiana, and additional members of this order came through Baltimore and progressed to Missouri, where they founded St. Mary's of the Barrens. Vincent de Paul's followers also had two foundations in the state of New York. One in Brooklyn became St. John's University, and the other, opened as a seminary, developed into Niagara University. By the mid-nineteenth century, Vincentians managed seminaries and colleges in Missouri, Louisiana, New York, Pennsylvania, Kentucky, and Ohio. In 1898, they also opened a high school in Chicago that eventually developed into DePaul University.

"Georgetown and St. Louis became the first Jesuit colleges and historians suggest that Jesuit influence may have been the strongest and most lasting."[1] From the Jesuit's early base at St. Louis University, in the early nineteenth century the order expanded its work along the Mississippi, Missouri, and Ohio rivers. The Jesuit concept of a college was that of the German gymnasium or French lycée, both of which consisted of six years, equivalent to four years of high school and two years of college. One example was Fordham University, which is the oldest Catholic institution of higher learning in the Northeast. It opened as St. John's in 1841 and was connected to St. Joseph's Seminary under Vincentian and diocesan clergy; it passed to the Jesuits shortly thereafter. By the twentieth century, the Jesuits had the largest network of colleges in the country, numbering about twenty-five.

The Franciscans' first permanent US establishment opened in Cincinnati in 1838. Twenty years later, they opened St. Bonaventure's College in Olean, New York, followed by the founding of St. Francis College, which was established in Brooklyn, New York.

The French Influence

Many communities of priests, brothers, and nuns were established in the early nineteenth century in the wake of the French Revolution. This spiritual movement is one of the most striking events in the recent history of the Catholic Church. In little more than a generation, a tremendous revival of religion took place in France. Many new religious orders were formed and many older ones were revitalized. While France experienced a great spiritual revival, our country, born of a revolution, benefited from the many Catholic orders that began as a result of another revolution. A number of congregations begun in France soon spread their influence to England, Ireland, and North America. The French religious congregations' contribution to the growth of American Catholic education was immense. The Vincentians and Sulpicians have already been mentioned. One must remember that nine of the thirty American bishops were French, and thus it was natural for them to turn to their homeland to call for help. Little did any of them know how enormous the response to their calls would be.

Notre Dame University was established in 1840 by the Congregation of the Holy Cross. Their founder, Basil Moreau, championed the importance of science and literature in the Catholic school curriculum. This congregation's unique contribution to American college life was residentiality, that is, the idea that the role of educators is not confined to the classroom but rather involves sharing their lives as well as their learning. Members of this congregation still live in college dormitories with students, where they lead discussion groups and conduct liturgies. Moreau's religious congregation was unique in the Catholic Church at the time, because it united priests and brothers in a single association that afforded equal rights and governing authority to both groups.

Five years after the de La Salle Christian Brothers arrived in New York from France in 1848 to staff the school of a French parish, they opened Manhattan College. During the Civil War, a partnership of Christian Brothers, diocesan priests, and laity opened La Salle University in Philadelphia. This new, collaborative approach was initiated under Bishop James Wood. The brothers taught in many elementary schools; in 1845, they opened Calvert Hall College High School in Baltimore, and they opened their first college in St. Louis in 1849. By 1873, about nine hundred brothers were teaching in more than one hundred schools, mostly boys' academies.

Initially, involvement in secondary education in America was a problem for the spiritual sons of de La Salle because they were prohibited from teaching Latin, a subject required by students as preparation for the university. Most of their schools had laymen teaching Latin as well as introducing modern languages and business, science, and engineering courses. The bishops in the dioceses that hosted the brothers' colleges directed them to teach the classics. The reward for the order was an increase in vocations from their students.[2]

William Joseph Chaminade, also of France, founded the Society of Mary, or the Marianists, in the early 1800s. Their educational activities are grounded on fundamental principles summarized as follows: "The spirit of faith helps a teacher to be truly present to students not only to teach them, but also to love and respect them. This causes students to change. An educator, personally transformed through faith of the heart, teaches students to be not only competent and capable, but also faithful and compassionate. As Mary formed her son Jesus, the Marianist educator fosters in each student and in each school the same love and mutual respect."[3] Chaminade, after his ordination, had to hide from the French authorities who were persecuting religious. The Marianists, composed of both brothers and priests committed to education, have been active in America since 1849. These sons of Mary founded St. Mary's School for Boys, which had developed into the University of Dayton by 1850. In 1852, Texas's first Catholic college, St. Mary's, was opened in San Antonio; it was eventually staffed by Marianists. Brothers and priests later arrived in Cincinnati to staff parish schools. By 1897, the Marianists had opened their first high school in St. Louis. The brothers eventually took over many primary schools throughout the country, and they are especially noted for their work among Germans. They opened Chaminade College in Hawaii in 1955.

Another French congregation, the Basilian Fathers, was established in 1822. As a result of the closing of seminaries during the French Revolution, two diocesan priests opened a secret school in the mountains of central France. After ten years, they bound themselves into a religious community dedicated to teaching and preaching. The Basilians were secular priests who lived in community and took a vow of poverty. Their order was slow in recruiting new members. These men agonized over the question of whether to be secular or religious priests. After they were invited to Toronto in 1852, the Basilians staffed a seminary in Ohio from 1867 to 1873, and they responded to American bishops who requested their services as educators. In the 1880s they extended their work to Detroit, and by the end of the century they were serving educational needs in Texas. The Basilian Fathers are dedicated to education. The American branch of the Basilians grew and eventually operated colleges and schools in Detroit, Texas, and later Rochester, New York.

The final French congregation discussed in this section is the Marist Brothers. They were founded by St. Marcellin Champagnat, who was upset by the lack of religion in the life of poor boys. In order to fill the need that he saw for boys' education, he founded the Marist Brothers and wrote a small book on the principles of teaching reading. His brothers taught diverse subjects, including religion, reading, arithmetic, principles of French grammar, Church music, and sacred history. Another addition Champagnat made to the curriculum was measurement, particularly calculations involving agricultural fields and properties—obviously useful considering the rural character of most of his schools.

The Institute of the Marist Brothers of Schools published "A Vision for Marist Education Today" in 1998. The work emphasizes the distinctive style of Marist education in the early nineteenth century. Some elements are: "Love for children, presence among the young, discipline as preventing faults and forestalling mistakes of the students, and developing the students' personal responsibility."[4] Years later, John Bosco also emphasized these as hallmarks of Salesian education.

A number of colleges continued to be founded by different orders in various parts of the country, and these formed a nationwide network of Catholic higher education that still exists. Dayton University (1850) and St. Mary's University in San Antonio (1852) were founded by the Marianists, Seton Hall (1856) was opened by diocesan clergy, and the de La Salle Christian Brothers opened a school for boys in Memphis in 1871 that is now Christian Brothers University. San Francisco's first college was the University of San Francisco, established by the Jesuits in 1855 as St. Ignatius Academy.

Non-Catholic colleges also grew with westward expansion. By 1860, there were 217 colleges, many located in the Midwest or Southwest. They provided rural people with the skills needed for urban occupations. After the Civil War, the number of Catholic colleges continued to rise. Duquesne (1878) was built by the Holy Ghost Fathers, Catholic University opened in 1887, St. Edward's was founded by Holy Cross brothers as the first chartered college in Texas in 1889, and St. Michael's Vermont (1904) was founded by the Society of St. Edmund.

Jesuit missionary Joseph Cataldo, working in the Rocky Mountains in the late 1800s, established boarding schools on reservations, recruited sisters and priests to staff them, and founded Gonzaga College as a boys' school that would allow native students to integrate with whites.

As religious communities took over the work of higher education in the latter half of the nineteenth century, bishops played a less active role in founding colleges. The exception was Seton Hall, which remained under diocesan control. There were fourteen Catholic men's colleges and universities in 1860; by the turn of the century there were sixty-three.

Colleges Become Universities

The colonial colleges were founded by English settlers with strong religious convictions; they wanted to ensure that religious customs would be preserved in their new country. When Georgetown, the first Catholic college, opened, fifteen of the seventeen established colleges had denominational roots. This trend continued through the first part of the nineteenth century—175 of the 182 colleges founded before the Civil War were affiliated with churches.

The basic purposes of the first Catholic colleges were similar to those of the other Christian schools; these included providing training for future priests, creating missionary centers, and cultivating moral virtues in young men. Unlike the Catholic elementary schools in which bishops played such an important role, it was religious congregations who founded and staffed most of these institutions of higher learning. By 1850, there were forty-two Catholic colleges, including Notre Dame (Holy Cross Fathers), Fordham (Jesuits), and Villanova (Augustinians). "Those colleges combined… while non-Catholic colleges followed the English model and separated the two."[5]

During the second half of the nineteenth century, what was taught and how it was taught at the colleges changed. At Notre Dame, Fr. Sorin decided that the original curriculum of his school, like the Holy Cross Fathers' college in France, was not adequately suited to American requirements. He wrote to Jesuits at Georgetown and St. Louis University, received information from them, and then revamped his academic program.[6] In the late nineteenth century, Catholic educational institutions began to change their attitude toward research, which up to that time was believed by many to have no place in Catholic education. Educators realized that emerging ideas in science, philosophy, and biblical studies posed the greatest challenge to the Catholic university.

Another motive for change came from the fact that educators became aware of the limitations of their approach. America used the German university as a model for change. As the denominational colleges moved their training for ministers to divinity schools, they expanded professional programs, such as those for medicine and law. "The British set precedents for undergraduate residential colleges, and the German institutions of higher learning expanded the teaching model to include formal lectures, laboratory techniques and emphasis on research. Yale conferred the first American PhD in 1861 and Johns Hopkins, founded in 1876, was the first institution to be established with emphasis on graduate work."[7]

At the end of the nineteenth century, Rev. James Burns commented that the progress in higher education made by Catholic colleges "had been great and rapid. The number of colleges and students had doubled in little more than a quarter century and the number of those doing post-graduate work had risen in the last thirty years from fewer than 200 to 5000. In 1800 in the US there were but 3 Catholic schools of theology, 3 of law and 3 medical. By 1900 there were 165 theology, 87 law and 56 medical."[8]

The Catholic University of America was one of the first three American institutions to dedicate itself to graduate study and research. The Catholic Sisters College, an adjunct to Catholic University, did the same for women. Bishop Spalding, in an address for Catholic University's cornerstone ceremony, stated that "pedagogy has grown to a science and chairs are founded in universities to expand the theory and art of teaching."[9]

The introduction of new courses or programs was a common phenomenon in American colleges in the post–Civil War period. The reason for this was the new demands placed upon colleges to prepare students for the diversity of professions and vocations in the growing American society.

Endnotes

1. Glazier and Shelly, editors (1997). *Encyclopedia of American Catholic History.* Collegeville, MN: The Liturgical Press, p. 251.

2. "St. John Baptist de La Salle." From www.newadvent.org/cathen/08444a.htm.

3. Glazier and Shelly, editors (1997). *Encyclopedia of American Catholic History.* Collegeville, MN: The Liturgical Press, pp. 840–841.

4. *In the Footsteps of Marcellin Champagnat: A Vision for Marist Education Today* (1998). Institute of the Marist Brothers of the Schools.

5. Patricia Hutchison (2001). *Purposes of American Catholic Higher Education: Changes and Challenges.* From http://www.newfoundations.com/History/Hutchison708F01.html.

6. Richard Sullivan (1951). *Notre Dame.* New York: Henry Holt and Co., p. 113.

7. Rena Foy (1968). *The World of Education.* New York: Collier Macmillan Ltd., p. 346.

8. https://www3.nd.edu/Departments/Maritain/etext/raae06.htm.

9. Glazier and Shelly, editors (1997). *Encyclopedia of American Catholic History.* Collegeville, MN: The Liturgical Press, pp. 308–309.

Other Sources

Harold Buetow (1985). *A History of United States Catholic Schooling*. Washington, DC: NCEA.

Matthew Bunson, editor (2001). *Catholic Almanac*. Indiana: Our Sunday Visitor Publishing.

Robert Burns (1999). *Being Catholic, Being American: The Notre Dame Story, 1842–1934*. Indiana: University of Notre Dame Press.

Lee Deighton, editor (1971). *Encyclopedia of Education, Vol. II*. Macmillan Company Free Press. Entry: Catholic Education in the United States, pp. 10-18.

D. Hollinger. *Positioning Secondary School Education in Developing Countries: Expansion and Curriculum*. Paper, David M. Kennedy Center for International Studies.

Hunt, Oldenski, and Wallace, editors (2000). *Catholic School Leadership: An Invitation to Lead*. New York: Falmer Press.

Catherine Kealey and Robert Kealey (2003). *On Their Shoulders: A Short Biographical History of American Catholic Schools*. Washington, DC: NCEA.

www.fms-sydney.org.

Theodore Maynard (1953). *The Catholic Church and the American Idea*. New York: Appleton-Century-Crofts Inc.

Charles Morris (1997). *American Catholic: The Saints and Sinners Who Built America's Most Powerful Church*. New York: Vintage.

Melanie Morey and John Piderit (2006). *Catholic Higher Education: A Culture in Crisis*. New York: Oxford University Press.

Timothy Walch (2003). *Parish School.* Washington, DC: NCEA.

Wilds and Lottich (1961). *The Foundations of Modern Education.* New York: Holt, Rinehart, and Winston.

Electronic Sources

"A Brief Overview of Catholic Schools in America." From www.ncea.org/newinfo/ncea.

"History of the Congregation of Holy Cross Brothers." From www.holycross.org/history/history.htm.

The Carmelites: Tradition: History: United States. From http://www.carmelites.net/about/history/.

"Characteristics of Marianist Education." From www.udayton.edu/smc/philfiles/cme2.htm.

"The Basilian Fathers." From www.sths.org/about/basilians.

"In the Basilian Way of Life." From www.basilian.org/publical/BWL/BWL1983/bwl77.htm.

"The Basilians: A Brief History." From www.basilian.org/publical/before/index.htm.

Marist Brothers. From www.fms-sydney.org.

CHAPTER 5

CATHOLIC EDUCATION IN THE NINETEENTH CENTURY

The Bishops

The Augustinians put down roots in the United States as early as 1796, when two friars from their Irish province founded St. Augustine Church in Philadelphia. One of the parish's more intellectual pastors later founded Villanova University. Many of the male orders trained their members to be teachers before the female orders, which were more focused on religious formation. Newly ordained priests would often spend a few years teaching before being assigned to regular parish work, and some diocesan priests remained in the classroom. The male religious communities also opened colleges earlier than the female communities, which at first opened theirs merely to train their novices.

As one reads the history of Catholic education, it becomes clear that an important factor in the growth of schools and the presence of religious to staff them was the bishop. The role and strength of Catholic education in each city and diocese depended on the degree of the bishop's belief in its importance.

As was noted earlier, Baltimore was the first diocese in the United States, established in 1789. Bishop John Carroll realized the importance of Catholic schools. At first, lay teachers staffed schools, but eventually they were joined by the Xaverian Brothers and the Brothers of St. Patrick.

Bishop Francis Kenrick of Philadelphia and Bishop John Hughes of New York "were so forceful as to become national leaders of the Catholic school movement."[1] In Philadelphia, Bishop Kenrick succeeded in having almost all of his city's churches open a school by the mid-nineteenth century. His successor, John Neumann, shared Kenrick's passion for educational work and was known for his development of elementary schools.

Bishop John Hughes of New York and others like him went to Europe to personally request that religious communities send missionaries to his city. In the early nineteenth century, a few lay-operated free schools existed in church basements in New York City. "During his tenure, Hughes established 25 new parochial schools. The Brothers of Christian Schools came in 1848 and in less than a 20 year period helped lay teachers in staffing the boys' departments of nine schools. Bishop Hughes was also responsible for bringing Jesuits to New York to take over what eventually became Fordham."[2]

As New York grew in size, the diocese was divided. When John Loughlin was consecrated the first bishop of New York's new diocese of Brooklyn in 1853, he began thirty-eight years of administration that resulted in the building of ninety-three schools, two colleges, and nineteen academies. During this time, he invited Franciscan brothers to join the Christian Brothers. His successor, Bishop McDonnell, also secured members of numerous orders, including the Benedictines, Redemptorists, and Capuchins. Decades later, during the first half of the twentieth century, Archbishop Malloy of Brooklyn doubled the number of both secondary and elementary schools in his diocese.

Most of the state of New Jersey was included in the diocese of New York until the diocese of Newark was initiated with Bishop Bayley as its leader. Bayley and Bishop Bernard McQuaid founded Seton Hall College in 1866, and the former served as its president.

Two years later, McQuaid was sent to the city of Rochester, New York. There he established a reputation as a leader who was deeply committed to Catholic education. In thirty years he opened twenty-six parishes and seventeen missions that included thirty parochial schools. McQuaid, who like many other bishops who supported education now has a Jesuit high school named after him, built vocational schools, seminaries, and at least seven high schools. "McQuaid's goal was to provide a free Catholic education to every child in the diocese. He was one of the first bishops to insist that all his schools meet state standards; students had to pass the New York Regents exams, and his teachers had to work toward certification."[3]

Even into the distant West Coast, the work of the bishop was a decisive factor. "Archbishop Charles Seghers, sometimes called the 'Apostle of Alaska', worked in Oregon City, established schools and parishes, and brought in Benedictines to assist in their administration."[4]

Early Problems for Catholic Education

So that one does not get the wrong impression, it should be pointed out that not all bishops agreed on the importance of Catholic education. For instance, St. Mary's was the first parochial school in Boston, and it was not opened until 1859. This highlights the different philosophy of that city's bishops with regard to Catholic education.

Another example is Bishop John Ireland, who led the diocese of St. Paul, Minnesota, after the Civil War. He was a scholar, but he didn't think that the Church could build schools quickly enough to keep pace with the rate of immigration. Also, he was somewhat philosophically opposed to ethnic Catholic schools because he believed that they delayed the immigrants' integration into American culture.

As time marched on and the Catholic immigrant population increased exponentially, there were some proposals drawn up to solve the problem of educating the Catholic population. One solution, called the Poughkeepsie Plan, permitted Catholic schools to be leased by the public board of education during school hours, and then they would revert to parish control later in the day. "The proposal drew protests because it did away with Catholic separatism and those like McQuaid felt that students educated in this environment would be less receptive to the Church. Disagreements between Protestants and Catholics prevented this possible solution from succeeding, and led to the Church's decree that parents support and send their children to Catholic schools."[5]

Growth of Catholic High Schools

As was true with the expansion of elementary education, the importance that bishops attached to Catholic education influenced the growth of high schools. When the twentieth century began, there were 183 Catholic colleges, all with preparatory schools.

One of the most noted names associated with Catholic secondary education was Bishop Doherty of Philadelphia. The first tuition-free Catholic high school for boys opened in Philadelphia in 1890. Parish pastors provided funding for the students. "This city was unique in the 1920s and 1930s for its extensive system of regional, diocesan run, tuition free central high schools, a model that was later widely copied throughout the country."[6] By 1951, the city boasted fifty-three schools staffed primarily by religious. Doherty also had 103 elementary schools in his diocese by 1903.

The rapid expansion of Catholic schools inevitably led to poorly trained teachers and crowded classrooms. "Msgr. John Bonner of Philadelphia, the long-time school superintendent, initiated many reforms including teacher training, improvements for physical plants [the buildings housing the schools], standardized testing and tracking, demonstration schools, master teachers programs, vocational training, guidance, and a greatly enriched curriculum. By the 1940s, Catholic high schools were offering aeronautics, mechanical drawing, and radio broadcasting."[7]

It was previously mentioned that in the mid-nineteenth century Boston was far behind many other cities in terms of the number of Catholic schools that were available for its residents. However, "There was a tremendous change in that arena during the second part of the nineteenth century and by 1907 the Boston diocese educated more than 50,000 Catholic students from elementary school to Boston College. Irish Catholics even controlled the public school system; it was noted that by 1930 half of Boston's principals were Catholic, most from the Jesuit's Boston College. In fact, the head of teacher development for the public schools was the sister of the priest in charge of teacher training at the college."[8]

Other cities noted for Catholic education included some farther west. In 1940, the archdiocese of Chicago boasted the largest Catholic school system in the world, with fifty thousand elementary students and twenty-eight thousand high school students.

In Los Angeles, during the post–World War II baby boom, Bishop McIntyre built almost two hundred schools and recruited sixty-eight religious orders for a multitude of services. During the decades following the mid-1950s, Catholics built almost two thousand new schools as the population became increasingly suburban and thus farther from the city center.

Endnotes

1. Timothy Walch (2003). *Parish School.* Washington, DC: NCEA, p. 32.

2. Thomas Shelly (2010). "Empire City Catholicism," in *Urban Catholic Education*, edited by Hunt and Walch. Notre Dame, IN: Alliance for Catholic Education Press, pp. 63-86.

3. Charles Morris (1997). *American Catholic: The Saints and Sinners Who Built America's Most Powerful Church.* New York: Vintage, p. 114.

4. Glazier and Shelly, editors (1997). *Encyclopedia of American Catholic History.* Collegeville, MN: The Liturgical Press, p. 1264.

5. Charles Morris (1997). *American Catholic: The Saints and Sinners Who Built America's Most Powerful Church.* New York: Vintage, p. 99.

6. Ibid., pp. 184–185.

7. Ibid., p. 185.

8. Ibid., p. 123.

Other Sources

Harold Buetow (1985). *A History of United States Catholic Schooling.* Washington, DC: NCEA.

Lee Deighton, editor (1971). *Encyclopedia of Education, Vol. II.* Macmillan Company Free Press. Entry: Catholic Education in the United States, pp. 10-18.

Catherine Kealey and Robert Kealey (2003). *On Their Shoulders: A Short Biographical History of American Catholic Schools.* Washington, DC: NCEA.

Theodore Maynard (1953). *The Catholic Church and the American Idea.* New York: Appleton-Century-Crofts Inc.

CHAPTER 6

BROTHERS, PRIESTS, AND CATHOLIC SECONDARY EDUCATION

Secondary Education

One of the difficulties of looking at the development of Catholic secondary education in America is that the schools were often closely associated with colleges. This practice continued for over a century and was changed only with difficulty. The development of Catholic education during the post–Civil War period incorporated the same changes as that of public schools, though at a slower pace. Staffing the schools required an influx of religious and serious recruiting of the students they taught. In many cases, it was the brothers and priests who accepted the responsibility of providing high school and college education for young men. Of course, they had been here already in small numbers, some teaching in parish schools, but their numbers increased in the late nineteenth century and early twentieth century. These orders grew in America because they found many vocations among the young men whom they taught.

While some religious communities of brothers were engaged in elementary education, for a time, most men in religious orders taught in the secondary level. Only after secondary education became more widespread and compulsory education laws were passed in the early decades of the twentieth century did priests and brothers become involved in Catholic schools in great numbers. "Some bishops developed the practice of assigning newly ordained priests to teach in high schools for a few years before beginning parish ministry."[1]

As the bishops were building schools in the large cities, many male religious orders were joining the sisters working on the frontier. For instance, Redemptorist priests came to New York in 1832 and started moving westward, establishing a school in Pittsburgh in 1839. Their work spread from that base.

In 1842, the Congregation of Holy Cross, founded by Basil Moreau, formed the first permanent establishment of brothers in the United States, at Notre Dame College. The conflicting feelings about college versus high school education were deeply felt by some religious leaders. For instance, when discussing Notre Dame after the death of its founder (Fr. Sorin), one author states that "the new president, Fr. Andrew Morrissey, neglected the university because his heart, and above all his mind, were with the prep school."[2] It was not until 1920 that the Notre Dame president, Fr. James Burns, eliminated the prep-school department from the college and gave the department's students over to the Sisters of Holy Cross.

The Congregation of Holy Cross, in addition to founding Notre Dame, started an agricultural school near New Orleans in 1859. Their brothers eventually concentrated on secondary education, and by the late 1960s they had sponsored thirty-three high schools.

The Carmelites' first steps in America were taken by Fr. Cyril Knoll, who came in response to a need for assistant priests in parishes in Louisville, Kentucky. Upon arriving, Fr. Knoll became aware of a shortage of priests available to serve German immigrants in the Midwest. As a result, the Carmelites opened a German parish in Kansas in 1869, and they later opened a school for boys. The Carmelite friars established their first American novitiate in 1866 in Maryland. By 1995, the Carmelites had over three hundred priests and twenty-three brothers administering six high schools, numerous parishes, and two retreat houses.

The Brothers of the Sacred Heart, founded by Pere Andre Coindre of Lyon, France, in 1821, had education as their charism and lived according to the Rule of St. Augustine. They managed schools, including commercial colleges, for boys. At roughly the same time that the Congregation of Holy Cross was establishing itself in Indiana, the Brothers of Sacred Heart went to Mobile, Alabama, and from that city spread throughout the United States and Canada. They were operating 150 schools, academies, colleges, and other institutions by the early twentieth century.

Meanwhile, in 1846, some Irish Brothers of St. Francis took over an elementary school in Loretto, Pennsylvania, that eventually became St. Francis University. They were active in other schools and were joined in 1858 by another group of Irish Franciscan brothers established in Brooklyn, New York. The sons of Francis also eventually expanded westward, establishing schools, including one college, in Nebraska and Minnesota.

Another group of educators who made an important contribution to Catholic education in America was the Congregation of Christian Brothers (also known as the Irish Christian Brothers), founded by Edmund Rice. He was married and had a daughter, whom he continued to care for while he worked as a religious educator. After his wife died, he organized a group of teachers to teach the poor children of Waterford, Ireland, and he eventually developed this group into a religious community. This group was influenced by the work being done by the Presentation nuns in the moral and religious education of poor girls. He opened his first school in Waterford in 1808, and he and six others made annual vows according to the rule and constitution of the Presentation order. They took vows of poverty, chastity, obedience, perseverance, and dedication to instruction of the poor. Edmund faced a difficult period when a new bishop seemed to oppose what he was doing. However, Edmund was given permission to establish his congregation as a pontifical order, and this allowed the brothers to move where they were needed. Some of his own brothers also challenged his authority.

Their first American foundation was a New York elementary school established in 1906. The greater part of the day in the brothers' schools was spent teaching material that would help poor boys succeed in a difficult and competitive society. They had an oral tradition rather than a formalized plan of studies, but their training led to a distinctive type of education that emphasized the importance of a mentor, Christian formation, and the need to overcome the students' lives of poverty. In 1909, they became involved in secondary education with the establishment of All Hallows Institute in New York. Rice's spiritual sons began a widespread system of secondary schools and opened Iona College in 1940. By the 1970s, the Christian Brothers staffed a number of diocesan high schools as well as their own institutions. As a growing population moved out to the suburbs, the brothers began to work with the more privileged.

The Presentation Brothers was the congregation composed of those who did not choose to become Irish Christian Brothers when given this option by the bishop of Conk. They moved to the United States during the twentieth century and established schools and missions in Pittsburg, Missouri, Arizona, Florida, and Tennessee.

Vocational Education

As was the case with the academic high schools that served as preparatory schools for the colleges, vocational schools grew during the latter half of the nineteenth century and continued to do so into the twentieth century. Before the Civil War and into the late nineteenth century, the American government funded missionaries to educate Native Americans. From the time of the earliest missions, Franciscans and Jesuits tried to train the Native Americans in various trades. The colonial form of vocational education was apprenticeship. Later, the government developed Protestant schools in addition to off-reservation boarding schools such as the Carlisle Indian School in Pennsylvania; these boarding schools included vocational instruction. During the latter half of the nineteenth century, different types of higher education developed; examples include agricultural colleges, institutes of technology, colleges for women, and universities. Meanwhile, the established colonial colleges became liberal arts colleges.

There were several religious congregations that assisted in offering vocational education to American youth in a Catholic environment. Theodore Ryken founded the Xaverians in Belgium in 1839 for the education of American youth. His earliest intention for the Xaverian Brothers was to train Native Americans. While doing catechetical work with Native Americans, Ryken realized that there were many immigrants who also needed help. At the request of the American bishops, he came to provide educational assistance. The Xaverians went to Kentucky in 1854 at the invitation of Bishop Martin John Spalding of Louisville, and they expanded their services to Baltimore in 1864. In addition to staffing parish schools, they opened St. Xavier's Institute, their first secondary school in America. By the late twentieth century, Xaverian-sponsored schools, including those with an emphasis on technical training, numbered twelve, located in the Northeast, Maryland, Kentucky, and Alabama.

Another vocational education-oriented order was the Salesians, once the third-largest teaching congregation after the Jesuits and Franciscans. They arrived in America in 1897 at the request of Bishop Corrigan of New York. Along with parish schools, they opened and staffed junior and senior high schools. The Salesians fostered their founder St. John Bosco's belief that technical schools were an excellent option for education, and they opened several across the country in the mid-twentieth century. John Bosco took what would now be called a holistic view of education, stressing the importance of school, church, playground (friends), and family. These four facets of the student were important to him because he believed that students could not learn unless they were loved and felt safe enough to express their feelings.[3]

The Salesians were trained to teach in a structured manner. "For the Salesians there was one point for each lesson followed by explanations of that point by members of the class. Texts were used for reference. . . . [Bosco] included works of the Church fathers in Latin rather than classics."[4] The study of music was a distinctive feature of his schools, and recreation was interspersed throughout the day. The role of the educator was important because Salesian educators were expected to be more than instructors. They were expected to be present, watching the students' activities so that they could better understand and therefore assist their students.

Since students were trained to be successful in an industrial society, the educator had to be a tradesman as well as an academic. "While Bosco had included St. Charles Borromeo's Sunday-school idea in the organization and administration of his Oratories, he had also learned from this well-known saint, the need for personal leadership and setting good example in time of crisis. . . . There was also an emphasis on youth or social work."[5]

There were also residential vocational schools that served several purposes. Brother Barnabas McDonald (1865–1929), a Christian Brother, taught elementary schools; later, after directing teenage retreats, he became involved in the care of delinquents and orphans. He supervised Lincoln Hall in New York, where he introduced a plan of family-like living units known as the cottage system, which was used in exclusive boarding schools. It became a model for child-care institutions throughout the country. If the concept sounds at all familiar, it is because his work is similar to that of Father Flanagan of Boys Town, who pioneered alternative education, vocational training, and self-government for homeless boys. "McDonald also established a special graduate course geared toward understanding boys at Notre Dame in 1924, as well as organizing adolescent guidance courses for volunteer welfare workers. He was nationally known for his work on adolescent development; even Presidents Theodore Roosevelt and Calvin Coolidge sought his advice on child welfare."[6]

The Role of Brothers in Education

Male religious orders began to train their personnel to teach in their schools before female religious orders did. This is perhaps attributable to the fact that male religious communities opened their own colleges earlier than female communities did. When female religious did build their colleges, they were restricted to educating future religious; only later did they offer entrance to laywomen. While the first boys' schools were seen as providing education for candidates for the priesthood, the girls' schools prepared their students for marriage and motherhood.

"Throughout much of the nineteenth century, the training of brothers as teachers in most of the orders of brothers was largely an apprenticeship model with some theory (usually philosophy and educational psychology) within the local community. In the case of the Irish Christian Brothers, following a year of induction into rules and practices of the community along with spiritual formation, there was a year of teacher preparation with supervised teachering, and then on appointment to a school, the brother was assigned a mentor teacher."[7]

The teaching brotherhood in the United States did not keep pace with the growth of female communities established in this country. Often brothers were recruited for the priesthood and as a result were removed from schools. Eventually, a shortage of brothers led even to sisters replacing brothers in all-male schools. In general, teaching brothers received half of what lay male teachers were paid, and nuns were paid half of what brothers made.

One writer, Rev. J.A. Burns (1912), describes how teaching brothers regarded their role in the education of adolescent males: "On their part the teaching brotherhoods have perceived that their main service is to be in the upper grades together with commercial and industrial training. This recognition led to more training for the brothers . . . a normal training of several years following upon and distinct from the novitiate."[8]

Between 1890 and 1930, the percentage of youth ages fourteen to seventeen in school increased from 4 percent to 47 percent. The concept of high schools changed during this period, from that of the college preparatory institution to that of a multifunctional institution. Topics included in the curriculum were health, family life, career/job training, citizenship, and use of leisure time. During those years, the junior high school also developed as an institution. After World War II, student populations of all educational levels, including the post-secondary level, increased dramatically.

Educators and pastors continued to add upper grades to parish schools to encourage children to prolong their education; this practice formed the foundation of the Catholic high school. As both more vocational schools and more academic high schools opened, the brothers and priests available for the classrooms could not meet the needs of Catholic schools' increasing enrollments. As one brother stated in the middle of the twentieth century,

> I sensed the dire need for teaching brothers and the tremendous influence for good which they can have. I heard our Bishops call them the hope of Catholic secondary education in America. . . . No wonder as I grew older, the statistics on the teaching brothers' strength in this country disturbed me—3,500 teaching brothers in the United States, as compared with 95,000 teaching sisters; 6,000 additional teaching brothers are needed by 1960 to meet the minimum needs of Catholic secondary education for boys.[9]

Although the Church did not favor co-education, the shortage of teaching brothers and the financial hardships associated with separate schools led to accepting co-ed schools and co-institutions when necessary. Co-institutional schools house a boys' division, supervised by male religious, and a girls' division, supervised by nuns. The divisions share common areas such as a gym, cafeteria, and library. By the late 1980s, about 43 percent of Catholic high schools were single-sex institutions, with boys enrolling in the most-advantaged schools and girls in the least-advantaged. Nuns taught the boys when priests and brothers were not available.

High School Curriculum

At the turn of the twentieth century, most Catholic schools were elementary. Only a few inter-parochial high schools, such as Roman Catholic High School of Philadelphia, had been established. Most high schools were administered by religious orders.

Secondary schools, especially those with a diocesan model, increased in number during the 1920s and 1930s. In 1936, Catholic sources reported 1,945 secondary schools with an enrollment of 284,736 students.

Changes occurred not only in who taught in these schools but also in what was taught. At first, secondary schools for males emphasized memorization, developed mental discipline, and created an elite group. One of the educational philosophies at the beginning of the twentieth century was called social traditionalism. Its followers believed that schools were supposed to prepare students for all phases of social life. "The Cardinal Principles of Secondary Education were an outcome of this school of thought and included the curricular importance of health, citizenship, command of fundamentals, vocation, home membership, and leisure."[10] "Although some Catholic high schools embraced the philosophy of the Cardinal Principles, this bulwark of the contemporary comprehensive public high school was eventually rejected by Catholics."[11] Support for maintaining traditional academic curricula came from Pius XI's encyclical *On the Christian Education of Youth*. He also emphasized the importance of single-sex schools. In 1912, Catholic colleges started implementing strict academic admissions standards so that the general public would hold them in higher regard. This practice pressured Catholic high schools to place the greatest emphasis on classical studies. According to research published later, "The colleges maintained close relationships with the boys' prep schools and the girls' academies, and tended to deprecate the weak academic programs in parochial and diocesan high schools. . . . To secure recognition and respect, diocesan schools increasingly put the college-prep curriculum first, with life studies becoming ancillary."[12]

During the twentieth century, Catholic high schools changed as they shifted from serving as one college's prep school to being independent schools serving local communities. For instance, construction of St. John's College Hall, in the Bushwick-Williamsburg district of Brooklyn, began in 1868. This was the forerunner of St. John's Prep and St. John's University. Although it opened in 1870, there was no distinction made between high school and college level studies until 1880. In 1927, Archbishop Malloy of Brooklyn opened a new preparatory school because of overcrowding. Saint John's Prep ended its affiliation with St. John's University in 1958, though it continued to operate under the Vincentians until the diocese took it over in 1972. The diocesan high school, Mater Christi—which opened in Astoria in 1961 and was staffed by the Sisters of Mercy and the Christian Brothers—was purchased by St. John's Prep, which moved to Astoria in 1981. In a similar way, Franciscan brothers came to Brooklyn from Ireland in 1858 and opened St. Francis Academy the following year. This academy became St. Francis College in 1884.

For the most part, all Catholic high schools of the twentieth century were educational communities that had much in common and that may even appear identical to the untrained eye. However, each had a different spirit, guided by the vision of the founder of the religious community that taught in that school. It was not only the leadership of the Roman Catholic principals but also the unique spirit of the founding fathers and mothers that permeated the buildings and campuses.

In 1903, the National Catholic Educational Association (NCEA) recommended that Catholics give as much importance to Catholic high schools as they did to grammar schools. As a result, the number of high schools increased dramatically beginning in 1920. Bishops took the lead in establishing area high schools to serve multiple parishes, and to provide for the management of these schools they created diocesan boards and appointed superintendents. The increasing numbers of graduates from these institutions created a need for more women's and men's colleges, leading to an increase in the number of such colleges that continued until the 1950s.

At the same time, vocational courses were gradually incorporated in public secondary schools. For example, English High School in Boston taught bookkeeping in 1823. A century later, business education was introduced into junior high schools to decrease dropout rates and make education more practical. The twentieth century witnessed the development of the comprehensive high school that incorporated practical and performing arts.

The need for secondary schools in America escalated throughout much of the twentieth century, and the de La Salle Christian Brothers answered the need for suburban high schools after World War II. As was true with the founders of female orders that came to America, de La Salle was flexible in adjusting the educational mission of his brothers to the needs of the people they served. As Theodore Maynard explains, "The Christian Brothers were founded in France to teach poor boys at schools that did not charge tuition. Latin was ruled out as being of no service to them; besides the founder did not want any of the Brothers to learn latin lest they should want to become priests."[13] When the brothers came to America, the rules were changed to charge tuition and to permit the teaching Latin.

Despite the shortage of teaching brothers and the financial hardship of providing separate schools for boys and girls, there were strong feelings against co-education. The most common form of compromise was the co-institution, in which separate schools operated in a common building and shared such resources as the library, cafeteria, and gym.

Peter Yorke's graded textbooks, based on the Baltimore Catechism and used in several California dioceses, were published in 1898 and later revised. They combined Bible history and catechism and were used in the schools operated by the Christian Brothers. Yorke's upper level books were related to the Manual of Christian Doctrine published by McVey in 1904. Catholic textbooks emphasized Catholics' continuing involvement in and contributions to American history.

In addition to preparing American Catholic youth to take their place in business and the professions, Catholic schools enabled a number of graduates to discern a religious vocation; often they would join the priests, brothers, or sisters who had educated them. In 1953, Maynard wrote that

> the best equipped and staffed seminary would be of no use if it did not have the right kind of boys in training for the priesthood. The priesthood and sisterhood can only be replenished by homes and schools. While it would be too much to say that everything would be lost if the parochial school were to disappear, certainly its disappearance would greatly hamper the Catholic Church. The Catholic ideal was that there would be a school connected with every parish—including a high school.[14]

At that time, Maynard made several observations about Catholic education. He noted that in the early 1950s, more secondary schools were needed and that there were major efforts under way to rectify the situation. He also pointed out that, "At this time, the Catholic schools are staffed by over 110,000 teachers of whom all but ten percent are sisters or brothers. The most important of the latter, the Christian Brothers [French], who at last began to charge tuition."[15] During the next ten years, more schools were built and staffed by an increasing percentage of lay teachers.[16]

"Los Angeles was the fastest growing diocese of the 1950s and 1960s. Archbishop James McIntyre built almost 200 schools. This was the last diocese to show such growth."[17]

As we begin the 2013–2014 school year, the NCEA reports that there are 5,399 Catholic elementary schools and 1,195 Catholic high schools. The staffing in these schools consists of 96.8 percent lay teachers, 2.2 percent sisters, 0.5 percent brothers, and 0.5 percent clergy.[18]

Endnotes

1. Catherine Kealey and Robert Kealey (2003). *On Their Shoulders: A Short Biographical History of American Catholic Schools*. Washington, DC: NCEA, p. 104.

2. Thomas Strich (1991). *My Notre Dame*. Indiana: University of Notre Dame Press, p. 14.

3. John Morrison (1979). *The Educational Philosophy of St. John Bosco*. New Rochelle, NY: Don Bosco Publications, p. 52.

4. Ibid., p. 73.

5. Ibid., p. 155.

6. Glazier and Shelly, editors (1997). *Encyclopedia of American Catholic History*. Collegeville, MN: The Liturgical Press.

7. Tom O'Donoghue (2012). *Catholic Teaching Brothers*. New York: Palgrave Macmillan, p. 107.

8. Bryk, Lee, and Holland (1993). *Catholic Schools and the Common Good*. Cambridge, MA: Harvard University Press, pp. 30–32.

9. Philip Harris (1954). "The Apostolate of the Modern Monk," in *Why I Became a Brother*, p. 171.

10. Bryk, Lee, and Holland (1993). *Catholic Schools and the Common Good*. Cambridge, MA: Harvard University Press, pp. 30–32.

11. Ibid.

12. Ibid.

13. Theodore Maynard (1953). *The Catholic Church and the American Idea*. New York: Appleton-Century-Crofts Inc., p. 232.

14. Ibid., p. 226.

15. Ibid., p. 233.

16. Ibid., p. 232.

17. Charles Morris (1997). *American Catholic: The Saints and Sinners Who Built America's Most Powerful Church*. New York: Vintage, p. 259.

18. www.ncea.org/data-information/catholic-school-data.

Other Sources

McDonald, pp. 308–309.

Carmelites, pp. 212–213.

http://www.xaverianbrothers.org/about-xb/who-we-are.

D. Hollinger. *Positioning Secondary School Education in Developing Countries: Expansion and Curriculum*. Paper, David M. Kennedy Center for International Studies.

Patricia Hutchison (2001). "The Purposes of American Catholic Higher Education: Changes and Challenges." From https://www.gonzaga.edu/academics/Graduate/Graduate-Student-Council/Catholic-HE.asp.

Edward Malloy (1999). *Monk's Reflections: A View from the Dome*. Kansas City: Andrews McMeel Publishing.

Arnoldo Pedrini (1987). *St. Francis de Sales: Don Bosco's Patron*. New Rochelle, NY: Don Bosco Publications.

Timothy Walch (2003). *Parish School*. Washington, DC: NCEA.

Electronic Sources

"History of the Congregation of Holy Cross Brothers." From www.holycross.org/history/history.htm.

The Carmelites: Tradition: History: United States. From http://www.carmelites.net/about/our-tradition/.

"Christian Brothers: Our Story." From http://www.iona.edu/about/history-mission/the-christian-brothers-story.aspx.

www.edmund-rice.wa.edu.au.

The Catholic Encyclopedia, copyright 1913 by Robert Appleton Co. Online edition, copyright 1999 by Kevin Knight. www.newadvent.org/cathen/. Entry: Christian Brothers of Ireland.

www.edmundrice.org.

CHAPTER 7

MOVING INTO THE THIRD MILLENNIUM

REACTING TO CHANGE

In the latter half of the twentieth century, the male orders began to re-evaluate their charisms.

A good friend of mine who accompanied me on my early-life journey through grammar and high school entered the Marist Brothers after our high school graduation. He taught high school while living in community after attending college and taking his final vows. Later, he worked with the poor, served as a residential chaplain at St. John's University, and presently is a vocation director for the Marist Brothers. He has not lived in community for a long period of time. Here are his thoughts:

> Because of my strong commitment to the Marist Brothers, I am in regular contact with them and am present at our celebrations and meetings. I have often said to them that I am sharing the richness of our community life and values with a wider population.... As I reflect on these past three years [as chaplain] I have never considered myself to be venturing

out on my own or separated from my community roots. For sure, religious life has always had individuals who moved beyond the so-called "cloister walls", mostly because they sought to bring the community's charism to a place where it was needed, and they believed their own individual talents and expertise—already shaped through the years—would benefit the people they served. . . . It is clear that today's world still welcomes the faithful creativity that religious life can offer.

"Those remaining in religious life were left with the challenge of the emphasis that the [Second Vatican Council] had placed on each religious order working out its charism, making the gospel their supreme rule and using the ideas and works of their founders to establish what should be distinctive about themselves and adapt it to contemporary life. This meant the prayer structure and daily schedule changed, as did their dress and freedom to use technology and transportation."[1]

While some decided to expand the services that they offered, others, such as the Jesuits, reaffirmed the importance of their secondary schools. In the United States, there are twenty-eight Jesuit colleges and universities and forty-six Jesuit high schools. In recent years, Jesuits along with members of the laity have created fourteen inner-city middle schools and five inner-city high schools. Cristo Rey is a national network of college-prep high schools in urban and low-income areas; an example is Cristo Rey Jesuit High School in Chicago. All schools in the program include a work-study component through which students finance much of their education. This program works closely with local businesses and affords students the opportunity to prepare for college while assisting their parents with tuition costs. Other orders and dioceses sponsor these schools in areas across the country; some examples include De La Salle North Catholic High School in Portland, Juan Diego Catholic Diocesan High School in Austin, and Verbum Dei High School in Los Angeles, which was founded by the Divine Word Missionaries.

Daniel Skala published a study in 1987 of the Xaverian Brothers and their schools in one province and found that changes in governmental procedures led to a new model in which the Brother Provincial serves as chairman of the board for all the schools and appoints a board of trustees composed of both brothers and laity.

Orders such as the Claretians, founded in Spain in 1849, have a special charism for assisting Hispanics. In addition to administering parishes in urban areas with large Hispanic populations, they are somewhat involved in education. For instance, they collaborate with Chicago schools and have initiated an institute where high school students no longer attending a public school can complete their education.

The late 1960s and 1970s saw the founding of four colleges with a staunchly conservative Catholic character: Christendom College in Virginia, Magdalen College and Thomas More College in New Hampshire, and Thomas Aquinas College in California. In 1990, Pope John Paul II issued *Ex Corde Ecclesiae* in an attempt to restore a degree of the Church's authority over Catholic higher education. Franciscan University in Ohio and Ave Maria University in Florida are the only full universities among the orthodox institutes.[2] New religious congregations and priestly fraternities—such as the Legionaries of Christ, founded by Fr. Marcial Maciel, and the Fraternity of St. Peter, established by Pope John Paul II—have started to make contributions to Catholic education. They both administer residential schools in Catholic settings.

Trends in Higher Education

As colleges felt the effects of a declining number of religious faculty during the latter half of the twentieth century, many Catholic colleges reoriented themselves. Common trends included accepting both men and women, combining with other Catholic institutions, and simply closing.

Universities are now in what is called the postmodern period. Many believe that their challenge is to adopt an interdisciplinary approach that puts theology on equal footing with other disciplines and that encourages research into the problems of our modern society. In *Ex Corde Ecclesiae*, Pope John Paul II wrote the following of Catholic institutions of higher learning: "Being both a university and Catholic, it must be both a community of scholars representing various branches of knowledge, and an academic institution in which Catholicism is vitally present and operative."[3] One answer to that dilemma may be found in the words of a former professor of Boston College, who in "The Catholic Intellectual Tradition in the Catholic University" reminds us that "a religiously based ethics should be the core of the Catholic university's professional school curriculum. We are the heirs and trustees of a great intellectual and cultural tradition founded on Christian faith and enhanced by grace and by many centuries of testing and authenticity."[4]

Another answer may be found in a late twentieth-century document. *Ex Corde Ecclesiae* identifies four characteristics that necessarily belong to research conducted by a Catholic university: the search for integration of knowledge, dialogue between faith and reason, ethical concern, and a theological perspective.

An interesting facet of university life at the end of the twentieth century was the role of institutes and centers in the educational process. "They are configurations of scholars, supported by funds from endowed, federal, or philanthropic sources, which undertake focused interdisciplinary research and scholarship."[5] Institutes do not generate courses like academic departments; an example is Notre Dame and its Cushwa Center for the Study of American Catholicism.

The institutes have also developed special programs to train new teachers. One such collaborative effort is the University Consortium for Catholic Education. The University of Notre Dame established a new model for Catholic teacher formation that has been adopted by other colleges.

As we continue through the second decade of the new millennium, there are approximately 265 Catholic institutions of higher education. Although there are fewer Catholic colleges now than in the past, their enrollments are high and there are even some new colleges opening. For instance, Magdalene College claims that it was established in the spirit of *Ex Corde Ecclesiae* and the Second Vatican Council. Located in New Hampshire and founded by laity in 1973, it offers a classical education. Another post-secondary institution, Ave Maria College, was established in 1998 by a lay board with the goal of advancing the ideals articulated in *Ex Corde Ecclesiae*. It is a liberal arts college committed to Catholic principles and to the formation of men and women in the intellectual and moral virtues of the Catholic Faith.

Making use of available technology, the Catholic Distance University, located in Virginia, offers undergraduate and graduate courses through distance learning. Its faculty is 25 percent religious and clergy who, along with their lay colleagues, represent most American dioceses and various international dioceses. So despite the problems that Catholic universities experienced in the latter half of the twentieth century, they are alive and well.

Not long ago, I was fortunate enough to have the opportunity to visit, through the hospitality of a former student, the University of Notre Dame. I returned home with many memories of the grotto and basilica, the excitement before the football game, and the sound of the band echoing through the campus. But one very memorable sight, which I had the forethought to take a picture of, was the reflection of the mural on the library wall in the pool that is at the foot of that building. A few years after I took that picture, I happened to be reading a book by Fr. Nicholas Ayo in which he describes the mural. He pointed out that it truly represents the mission of the Catholic university: "One looks into this pool of clear water and one sees the face of Christ, who is the unique Word of God and the everlasting truth. He is surrounded in the mural by the sages of Christianity, the saints and mystics, the philosophers and the theologians, the learned men of yesteryear east and west. . . . Here is God with us. Here is the fullness of truth that the books of the library but seek."[6]

Endnotes

1. Tom O'Donoghue (2012). *Catholic Teaching Brothers.* New York: Palgrave Macmillan, p. 132.

2. "Who is Catholic?" *The Chronicle*, April 9, 2004.

3. Pope John Paul II (1990). *Ex Corde Ecclesiae*, no. 14, in *Catholic Universities in Church and Society: A Dialogue on Ex Corde Ecclesiae*, edited by John P. Langan (1993), Washington, DC: Georgetown University Press, p. 235.

4. Monica Hellwig (2000). "The Catholic Intellectual Tradition in the Catholic University," published in *Examining the Catholic Tradition*, edited by Anthony Cernera and Oliver Morgan. Fairfield, Conn.: Sacred Heart University Press.

5. Edward Malloy (1999). *Monk's Reflections: A View from the Dome.* Kansas City: Andrews McMeel Publishing, p. 104.

6. Nicholas Ayo (2001). *Signs of Grace: Meditations on the Notre Dame Campus*. Lanham, MD: Rowman & Littlefield Publishers, p. 70.

Other Sources

Timothy J. Cook (2002). *Architects of Catholic Culture*. Washington, DC: NCEA.

John Fialka (2003). *Sisters: Catholic Nuns and the Making of America*. St. Martin's Press.

Richard M. Jacobs (2001). *The Vocation of the Catholic Educator*. Washington, DC: NCEA.

G. Kearney (2008). *More Than a Dream: The Cristo Rey Story*. Loyola Press.

Catherine Kealey and Robert Kealey (2003). *On Their Shoulders: A Short Biographical History of American Catholic Schools*. Washington, DC: NCEA.

Mary McDonald. "The Catholic School on the Threshold of the Third Millennium." *Momentum*, September/October 2000, pp. 23–24.

Electronic Sources

www.con.org. On Catholic universities.

www.legionairesofchrist.org

www.fssp.org

United States Conference of Catholic Bishops. From www.usccb.org

http://www1.villanova.edu/villanova/mission/heritage/values.html

http://www.cdu.edu/about/history

"Missionaries of the New Millennium." http://cdom.org/schools/jubileeschools/missionaries.htm.

Arthur Jones. "Catholic Colleges and Universities: Preserving Mission and Ministry at College." From www.natcath.com/NCR_Online/archives/102502/102502u.htm.

Boston College. "A Pocket Guide to Jesuit Education." From www.bc.edu/offices/mission/publications/guide/success.

www.universityofsacramento.org/html/history.html

www.claretians.org/about-us

www.schools.archdiocese-chgo.org/news_releaes/news_2003/news_050203.shtm

www.shupress.sacredheart.edu/ECIT/hellwig1.htm

"Sharing Catholic Social Teaching: Challenges and Directions, Reflections of the US Catholic Bishops." From http://www.usccb.org/issues-and-action/human-life-and-dignity/index.cfm.

www.mi.avemaria.edu/about/overview.html

www.magdalen.edu

CHAPTER 8

THE TWENTY-FIRST CENTURY AND THE FUTURE

The Heritage of the Male Institutes

Each of the male religious orders—whether Jesuit, Marist, Marianist, Christian Brother, Benedictine, Dominican, Franciscan, Augustinian, Basilian, Salesian, or Xaverian—still has some schools open throughout the United States, although there may not be many brothers or priests in the administration or on the staff. Young men in cities, suburbs, and rural areas continue to be educated in the distinctive culture of these schools. The Jesuit schools may emphasize the *Spiritual Exercises* and teach through a modern adaptation of the *Ratio*, the Benedictine schools have evidence of hospitality, community, and meditation, and the Marist and Marianist schools place particular emphasis on the Blessed Mother; nevertheless, all of these Catholic schools have much in common.

All value the relationships that educators form with students. It is through these more personal encounters that Christ's presence is brought to the classroom, stage, gym, and playing field. John Bosco, John Baptist de La Salle, and Marcellin Champagnat all emphasized the importance of taking a personal interest in students and trying to keep them out of trouble. While this philosophy may not have been given a particular label—John Bosco called it "preventive discipline"—all agreed on its importance.

As one reviews the writings of the founders and reads the instructions they gave to their followers, one notices the importance of teachers who have the virtues of humility, patience, fairness, kindness, and charity, among others. John Baptist de La Salle wrote a lengthy document listing and explaining all of the virtues that a teacher should have. Modern documents on Catholic education still list and explain similar virtues that lay teachers should strive to practice. Contrary to stories of corporal punishment that supposedly took place in these schools decades ago, founders such as Marcellin Champagnat, John Baptist de La Salle, Chaminade, and John Bosco all warn against punishing students out of anger or as physical retribution. These men recognized the damage that teachers can cause when they lose control of themselves. They agree that students learn more through love and kindness than through fear. This in no way diminishes the value of running orderly schools, where students know how to act properly and what is expected of them. Understanding the weakness of all men, and the developmental stages that adolescents progress through, the founders all justify the use of some type of code of conduct that spells out the consequences of doing something wrong.

Their writings on school leadership reflect their values. Leaders of Benedictine schools should embody the virtues of an abbot—displaying hospitality, correcting and admonishing gently. Principals are expected to create communities of learning, a term now frequently used in secular schools, to foster Catholic values.

For some orders, their values developed gradually; the Marist and Christian Brothers, for example, began by opening elementary schools for poor boys in France and other countries. Edmund Rice, founder of the Irish Christian Brothers, did the same in Ireland. The Jesuits, though they never operated elementary schools, have a long history of educating young men in high schools and colleges. Even with the differences in the age groups they worked with, all teaching orders had the same theological heritage in terms of the importance of the Eucharist, the other sacraments, prayer life, and community. In recent times, teaching orders have emphasized the importance of community service, justice, and preference for the poor. The canned-food collections of the young and the local community service of high school students lead to the national and international service work of college students and university graduates.

Some orders, such as the mendicant orders and the Benedictines, began with different purposes but then gravitated toward education. The Benedictines are still a monastic order devoted to prayer and work. The work began as manual labor, and for many Benedictines it still is, but other types of labor became important as the schools they established to teach potential novices developed into schools for laity. The Dominicans, whose purpose is found in their name—the Order of Preachers—found a number of their members in universities, interpreting preaching as teaching. The Franciscans did not have a smooth transition to classrooms because their original charism of begging and poverty forbade the ownership of books, and the early members looked upon scholarship as something that diverted attention from prayer. Eventually, members of these congregations, along with Augustinians, had schools associated with universities, and their clergy were professors or even held chairs of departments. All of the original universities in Europe were Catholic institutions, and they remained so until the time of the Reformation.

Teachers in Catholic schools have a rich heritage to learn from. Catholic founders and educators had many ideas about education that are still important and vital. John Baptist de La Salle and Marcellin Champagnat emphasized that their brothers must be watchful over their students. John Bosco served as a model for the personal relationships that the educator can develop with his or her students.

Most importantly, they teach what my pastor has called the unique Catholic vision: Christ is made manifest through us in the bits and pieces of each day. The fact that we can walk away from the altar in the morning and bring Christ to others through our presence is an important facet of the lens through which the Catholic looks at the world.

"For schools sponsored by religious congregations, core beliefs and values reflect the charism of the sponsoring religious community."[1] Jesuit schools stress reflection and service to others, while the schools of the Sacred Heart brothers are built on principles of personal and active faith in God, deep respect for intellectual values, and personal growth in an atmosphere of wise freedom.

Although the religious in schools are now few in number, their presence reminds students that there are choices in life: choices that involve how one lives, what one believes to be important, and how happiness, religion, and an occupation or vocation are connected. The vows of religious teachers, rather than separating them from those in the world, free them to serve God and those with whom they work.

Lay Teachers

The lay teacher in a Catholic school, while not living religious vows, also represents to the student a way to live in the world and yet bring a Christian presence into it. The lay teacher should embody the values of the Church and the school, and teach through relationships. The difference is that he or she may be married, may have a family, and may need to supplement his or her income.

Vatican Council II reiterated that what makes the Catholic school distinctive is its religious dimension, and that this dimension should be found in the educational climate, the personal development of each student, the relationship established between culture and the Gospel, and the illumination of all knowledge with the light of faith. The *Declaration on Christian Education* (1965), acknowledges all of the problems that our society presents to youth. The difficulties of poverty, single-parent families, choices youth must make about substance abuse and sex, and violence all make clear the importance of an education that is grounded in a Catholic philosophy of life. Central to these issues is the teacher. The *Declaration on Christian Education* speaks of the importance of the relationship between teachers and students in Catholic schools and the need for administrators to continue to ensure that the schools are true communities in which the student feels valued and cared for. It also suggests that teachers should share their own spiritual lives and the prayers that they offer for the students entrusted to them.

All Catholic-school teachers should seek to continue and expand upon the social consciousness initiated by Pope John XXIII through his concerns about inequity with regard to the distribution of the world's economic resources and about the numerous people living under tyrannical rulers. They should encourage students to conduct fundraisers for the needy, to engage in volunteer work, and, at the college level, even to dedicate a year or two of their lives after graduation to working with the disadvantaged throughout the world. In addition, emphasizing the importance of the social responsibility that students have must be part of the culture of any Catholic school.

In 1929, Pope Pius XI synthesized Catholic educational thought in his encyclical *On the Christian Education of Youth*, in which he stressed the importance of teachers who combine their intellectual talents and moral qualifications with their love of students. Years later, Pope Pius XII asserted that God's love for youth is communicated through the relationships that educators forge with their students. It is the teacher's moral quality that motivates students to imitate their teacher's example. "The vocation of the Catholic educator is God's call to the educator's heart; a divine summons to devote one's talents and energies to enable youth to understand their mission to continue building God's kingdom. Within the context of an intimate conversation between each educator and student, a relationship characterized by Christian personalism, young men and women come to recognize the Lord Jesus living and acting in their midst."[2]

Educational theories changed greatly during the century following John Bosco's work, but even in 1971 Henri Nouwen, author of *Creative Ministry*, wrote, "Perhaps we have paid too much attention to the content of teaching without realizing that the teaching relationship is the most important factor. It is a relationship that is beneficial for the teacher as well as the student."[3]

In *The Risk of Education*, Luigi Giussani states why this is so: "Our relationship to Christ passes through people who enter into relationships with one another." He poses the question, "How can we keep being young?" His reply is the following:

> During the period when student and teacher share the same experience working side by side, that teacher lives a life that as time goes by, maintains its youthful attitude, remains open to learning and is filled with wonder and moved by things. These are the elements I would still select to construct a formula for everlasting youth. The connections made by good teachers are held not in their methods but in their hearts—meaning heart in an ancient sense, as the place where intellect and emotion and spirit will converge in the human self.[4]

Endnotes

1. Timothy J. Cook (2002). *Architects of Catholic Culture.* Washington, DC: NCEA, p. 19.

2. Richard M. Jacobs (2001). *The Vocation of the Catholic Educator.* Washington, DC: NCEA, p. 43.

3. Henri Nouwen (2003). *Creative Ministry.* New York: Image Books, p. 11.

4. Luigi Giussani (2001). *The Risk of Education.* New York: Crossroad Publishing, p. 46.

Other Sources

Lillie Albert. "The Call to Teach: Spirituality and Intellectual Life." From http://64.226.189.222/collegium/albert.htm.

http://www.marquette.edu/library/conversations/No18_2000/No18_albert.PDF.

Richard Liddy (2000). "Spirituality and the Academic Vocation" from the proceedings of the Center for Catholic Studies. "I Have Called You by Name: Spirituality and the Academic Vocation," Summer Seminar 2000, Seton Hall University, South Orange, New Jersey.

CHAPTER 9

SISTERS: PARTNERS IN AMERICAN EDUCATION

Background

Women also have made, and continue to make, tremendous contributions to Catholic education in America. Nuns can be traced to communities of women in the third century. In 325, St. Pachomis built a monastery for his sister and her companions, and St. Basil began one for his sister Macrina and her colleagues.

In early times, nuns provided Christian education to young girls, especially those training for religious life. Monasteries for women began to be formed in Western Europe in the fifth century; one of the first was founded by St. Patrick. Each of the mendicant orders had convents of women associated with them. "The new religious societies of women tended toward apostolic work, unlike their predecessors, who mostly devoted themselves exclusively to prayer and contemplation. Examples include the Ursulines, who were founded in Italy by Angela Merici in 1535, and the Daughters of Charity who were established in Paris in 1660 by St. Louise de Marillac."[1] These groups were not alone in their work. The Visitation order, founded by St. Francis de Sales and St. Jane Frances de Chantal, placed emphasis on teaching girls. The paths of members of each of these orders would cross in a new nation, and together they would contribute to building a network of schools unlike any that had yet been seen.

Sisters Come to America

Religious congregations of women began contributing to the formation of the Church in the United States when Ursuline nuns came to the French colony of New Orleans in 1727. They began a pattern continued by later congregations when they opened an academy for girls and a free school for blacks and Native Americans. Other religious who arrived at our shores during the next two hundred years often did so in answer to American bishops' requests for help.

Catholic education in eighteenth- and nineteenth-century America was influenced by the fact that female religious, unlike their male counterparts, founded their own orders of sisters or initiated congregations of already existing European orders; the members of these congregations were known as sisters or daughters. An example of an American order that originated from a European order was the Daughters of Charity. In Europe, St. Vincent de Paul and St. Louise de Marillac founded the Ladies of Charity, sometimes called Vincentian women. The charism of the Ladies of Charity is to adjust the missionary focus of the order so as to address unmet needs in new ways.

Louise de Marillac developed the foundation for the work of her American daughters by advocating the education of young girls, providing training for teachers, teaching, and preparing lay catechists. She was also particularly interested in early-childhood training. "De Marillac drafted the 'Particular Rules for Schoolmistresses', which became the basis for Vincentian women educators, including the Sisters of Charity who taught Catherine Harkins-Drake in Pennsylvania. De Marillac, who composed her own catechism, established a normal school for teacher training at the motherhouse and a laboratory school where the novice sisters did their practice teaching. Elizabeth Seton would later imitate this practice."[2]

American Congregations

During the closing years of the eighteenth century, Elizabeth Seton, a mother and convert to Catholicism, founded a small boarding school for girls in Baltimore, next to the Sulpicians' seminary at St. Mary's. It was a combination boarding and free school. The combined efforts of the Sulpician priests, Archbishop Carroll, and St. Elizabeth led to the formation of the first order of sisters founded in America.

Timothy Walch tells us that "the ability of Catholics to staff parish schools was aided substantially by Seton. It was her vision of an order of teaching sisters that became the framework for the growth of Catholic schooling."[3] The sisters later established the College of Mount St. Vincent, which, along with the cathedral school at St. Patrick's, offered education to New York youth.

Catherine Harkins-Drake, who was born in Ireland, became the founding president of the Ladies of Charity of St. Louis in 1857. For both Elizabeth and Louise, relationships with those they trained were important.

Coincident with Seton's work, a group known as the "Pious Ladies of Georgetown," led by Alice Lalor, assisted the Poor Clares in running a school and made initial vows as Visitation sisters. In 1799, Lalor founded Georgetown Visitation Prep for girls, establishing a new convent of the Sisters of the Visitation as well as an academy for girls in Virginia. In 1834, Visitation nuns established an academy at Summerville, Alabama. When the Louisiana Purchase doubled the size of the American diocese in 1805, these sisters built schools east of the Mississippi and then moved west with the settlers.

John Carroll, while petitioning for more dioceses to be created, asked some of the religious orders to follow settlers as they moved westward. As a result, Reverend Charles Nerinckx, assisted by Mary Rhodes, founded the Sisters of Loretto at the Foot of the Cross in Kentucky during 1812. Ten years later, the Dominicans also opened a motherhouse in Kentucky and would later open many academies and one college in the Midwest. When Fr. Benedict Flaget, a friend of Mother Seton, was named bishop in Kentucky, Seton's sisters began a congregation there, the Sisters of Charity of Nazareth. Catherine Spalding was their first superior, and a university bearing her name now stands in Louisville. In 1824, they opened St. Clare's Academy in Vincennes.

Another noted American founder of the period was Mother Mary Elizabeth Lange, who founded the Oblate Sisters of Providence in 1828. Their mission was to educate blacks. She opened a school in Baltimore, but her community faced much opposition from the city's citizens throughout the mid-nineteenth century. One of the sisters of this community, Theresa Maxis Duchemin, later left the community and founded the Servants of the Immaculate Heart of Mary. Her congregation eventually staffed and founded many Catholic schools in Pennsylvania. Meanwhile, Mother Lange succeeded in founding schools in Philadelphia, New Orleans, and St. Louis.

French Congregations

As was true for priests and brothers, teaching sisters brought a distinctive French religious influence into our schools. The Sisters of St. Joseph—founded by Fr. Pierre Medaille, SJ, in 1650 and reorganized by Sister St. John Fontbonne after the French Revolution—came to St. Louis and expanded as the American frontier grew, staffing schools, hospitals, orphanages, and homes for the elderly. Under Mother St. John they would become the second-largest congregation in the United States.

There are many other examples of French congregations. Madeleine-Sophie Barat founded the Society of the Sacred Heart of Jesus in November 1800. "They take vows of poverty, chastity, obedience, stability, and dedication to teaching young women. They live by the Jesuit rule. Barat presented the congregation *The Plan of Studies* in 1805 that was heavily influenced by the *Ratio Studiorum*. It was revised through the years in order to meet the needs of the educational ideals of different countries. *The Plan* lays particular stress on history, literature, writing, world languages, and household management."[4] Philippine Duchesne introduced the Sacred Heart Sisters into America in 1818. Their first houses were in Missouri and Louisiana. The sisters established the first free school west of the Mississippi, teaching Creole, French, and American students. They also opened convent schools, boarding schools for upper-class youngsters, and novitiates.

While the number of congregations that arrived in our country may lead one to believe that these women did not face obstacles, the opposite is actually true. For instance, St. Julie Billiart suffered from debilitating diseases most of her life. She founded the Sisters of Notre Dame de Namur in France in 1803 to teach girls and train religious teachers. Because their French bishop didn't like the terms of their rule, they moved to Belgium. Sister Louise Schrieck went to Cincinnati with a group of Notre Dame sisters in 1840 and "articulated the system of education introduced by Sister Julie Billiart and refined by Francois Blin de Bourbon."[5] In addition to teaching immigrants in Ohio and on the East Coast, they taught wealthier boarders and day students in academies as well as thousands of Sunday-school students. The sisters are particularly known for educating both boys and girls in all of the secular subjects. Their system of education, as is true for a number of teaching orders, is based on that of John Baptist de La Salle. They are also noted for their use of the wooden clapper in giving directions for movements in class; the constant presence of the teacher with her class, whether in the classroom or in recreation areas. They also taught vocal music, drawing, and needlework. The Sisters of Notre Dame later opened schools in Toledo, Ohio; Boston; Washington, D.C.; and Oregon.

The sisters encountered a variety of problems. Marguerite Bourgeoys (1620–1700) went as a lay teacher to Montreal, Canada, where she founded the Sisters of the Congregation of Notre Dame for the education of native peoples and girls. In 1864, this congregation opened an academy in Portland, Maine. She reported that a bishop tried to force enclosure upon them and thus prevent the sisters from teaching. A fire later destroyed her convent, resulting in the deaths of two of her sisters. Several other groups entered the United States from Canada, led by determined women who did whatever was necessary to provide education. Mother Joseph of the Sacred Heart, from the Sisters of Providence in Canada, traveled to the Washington Territory and over forty-six years built seven academies and five Native American schools in addition to hospitals and orphanages. She is esteemed as the first architect of the Pacific Northwest.

The Sisters of Charity of Providence opened Providence Academy, which was the first permanent school in the Northwest. Sister of Providence Esther Pariseau was considered the architect of many schools in the Northwest, where she oversaw design, construction, and fundraising for Providence institutions.

Immigration and Additional Congregations

As immigration became a driving social and religious force during the nineteenth century, American bishops increasingly turned to Europe for assistance in working with recent arrivals from Ireland, Germany, and Italy. Not all such requests for assistance were responded to in an affirmative manner. In the mid-nineteenth century, when John Neumann of Philadelphia asked the pope to send German Dominicans to his diocese, he was advised to establish a congregation of Franciscan sisters instead. So in 1855, the bishop, along with a widow named Mary Francis Bachmann and some of her companions, founded the Sisters of St. Francis of Philadelphia. They responded to the need for teachers at parish schools in Philadelphia; went to Syracuse, New York, at the request of Franciscan friars, to teach German immigrant children; and established schools in western cities, including Baker City, Oregon.

Many Catholic bishops had gone to Ireland seeking nuns. The Sisters of Mercy, under the leadership of Frances Ward, came from Ireland in 1843, and the Servants of the Immaculate Heart of Mary, founded by Theresa Duchemin in 1845, started schools in Michigan. By 1852, Catholic sisters from various congregations had created 133 schools, mostly for women.

One of the most productive female religious congregations was the Sisters of Mercy. "Catherine McCauley founded the Sisters of Mercy, a Catholic religious order that has founded more schools than any other religious order in the English speaking world. In 1858 the Sisters of Mercy began to teach at St. Anne's, Manchester, New Hampshire. By 1881, after only thirty-eight years in America, the ranks of the Mercies had grown to ten thousand sisters."[6]

Unlike most of their predecessors, Mary Frances Clarke and four of her friends were not nuns when they left their home country; they came from Dublin in 1833 to teach children of Irish immigrants in Philadelphia. There they established Miss Clarke's Seminary for poor girls from Dublin. Clarke's group formed the Sisters of Charity of the Blessed Virgin Mary at the end of that year, and eventually they found their way to San Francisco, where they started a school in 1887.

The Sisters of the Presentation of the Blessed Virgin Mary were founded by Honora Nagle (1718–1784) in Ireland; they joined the Irish Christian Brothers, who also served the needs of Irish immigrants. They responded to the call of priests from the far West in 1854, traveling to San Francisco. Later, others went to New York City, the Dakotas, and Dubuque, Iowa.

French, German, and Irish orders found new life in the first half of the nineteenth century after facing suppression of the Catholic Church by the ruling governments in each of their countries. It was in this culture that Caroline Gerhardinger, later called Mary Theresa of Jesus, founded the German congregation of the School Sisters of Notre Dame in 1833.

The School Sisters of Notre Dame later traveled by stagecoach and steamboat to Mississippi, and once there, they met the needs of girls in elementary schools and also established some vocational schools and orphanages. As their work spread, the sisters accepted non-Germans into their order and taught in schools composed of boys and girls from a variety of ethnic groups. By the turn of the twentieth century, they formed the largest congregation of female religious in the United States. They trained future teachers and pioneered the development of kindergartens.

Carmelites, Bavarian Benedictines, and Dominicans joined their male counterparts in America and took their places among the largest teaching orders. The Sisters of St. Benedict arrived in the United States in 1852 to teach

German students. Switzerland and Bavaria provided most of the Benedictines, both men and women, who came to America in the early years.

A foundation of Dominicans in Ratisbon, Germany—they were strictly cloistered until the beginning of the nineteenth century, at which time they started teaching—sent four sisters to Brooklyn, New York, in 1853. From there, the congregation spread throughout the country and opened academies for girls. By 1964, they managed forty-six high schools and four colleges in addition to over two hundred elementary schools.

Polish immigration took place in the late nineteenth century and early twentieth century. The first Polish order to establish itself in the United States was the Felician Sisters, also known as the Congregation of the Sisters of St. Felix. Asked to come to Wisconsin in 1874 by Fr. Dabrowski, he and the sisters wrote and printed forty-five different books, and Dabrowski taught the postulants all academic disciplines.

The largest Polish population outside of Poland was in Chicago. Blessed Frances Siedliska, founder of the Sisters of the Holy Family of Nazareth from Poland, came to the United States with sisters in 1885 to establish a foundation in that Midwestern city. The sisters were devoted to Christian education and other charitable works. The Sisters of the Resurrection and the Polish Sisters of St. Joseph followed them.

In the late 1800s, Italians formed the largest group of immigrants. Mother Francesca Cabrini of the Missionaries of the Sacred Heart answered the call of Pope Leo XIII, who requested that Cabrini's sisters undertake service to immigrants in the United States. Her sisters opened schools in many parishes and taught in Italian. She founded Mother Cabrini High School, which was originally opened for wealthy Italian girls. The sisters also opened industrial schools where embroidery and other practical arts were taught.

Another Italian saint whose sisters contributed to American education was St. Lucy Filippini, who was cofounder of the Religious Teachers Filippini. They developed into one of the great teaching orders of Italy. The sisters responded to the call of the bishop of Newark, New Jersey, in 1919; he asked them to teach in the parish schools. By 1960, the community numbered over five hundred sisters teaching fifty thousand first- and second-generation Italian Americans.

Another order that was closely related to Italian immigrants was the Salesian Sisters of St. John Bosco, cofounded by St. Mary Mazzarello. They established themselves in the United States by working closely with Salesian priests in Paterson, New Jersey, in 1908. When the congregation was founded by St. John Bosco and St. Mary, they adjusted the preventive system that Bosco had initiated for boys so that it would also be beneficial for girls.

Academies and Catholic Higher Education for Young Women

Immigration caused the Catholic population to grow, and colleges were opened for the daughters of Catholic families that also afforded higher education for nuns. In Europe, unlike in America, there were training colleges for primary teachers sponsored by many of the same orders found in the United States, including the Sisters of Notre Dame de Namur, the Sisters of the Sacred Heart, and the Sisters of Mercy. The Sisters of Notre Dame de Namur and the Sisters of the Holy Child Jesus managed the best-known training colleges for secondary teachers.

As our country's settlers moved west, a trail of colleges followed. For instance, the Sisters of Charity of Nazareth in Kentucky opened Spalding College in 1814. In the 1840s, the Sisters of Charity opened Dubuque College and Clarke College in Iowa, and the Sisters of Providence opened Saint

Mary-of-the-Woods College for women in Indiana. Saint Mary's (1860) was established at Notre Dame by the Sisters of Holy Cross, and St. Xavier (1847) was established in Chicago by the Sisters of Mercy; also maintaining a strong presence in colleges were the Sisters of Notre Dame and the Benedictines.

At the turn of the twentieth century, colleges for Catholic women developed more slowly than those for men, though other private women's colleges such as Vassar and Wellesley were available.

Changes in society made it important for young men to receive a complete education, and such changes eventually did the same for young women. Of course, this development called for the assistance of many more sisters, including the Daughters of Wisdom from France.

In Philadelphia, the first free central Catholic high school in the United States opened in 1890. One for girls opened in that same city eighteen years later. Schools and academies were different: schools were co-ed, although initially boys and girls were kept separate. In the schools, the sisters taught the basic subjects of reading, writing, arithmetic, religion, history, and geography. They were roughly the equivalent of primary schools.

Girls' academies, which corresponded to high schools, were academically rigorous, especially those run by Mother Duchesne's Society of the Sacred Heart. Their curriculum included philosophy, Bible history, rhetoric, chemistry, and Christian ethics. There were over seven hundred girls' academies in 1910.

The Sacred Heart nuns, in addition to running prestigious schools for girls, educated thousands of boys in parish schools. They also established ten college level institutes for women. The Holy Child sisters from England also made major contributions to secondary and college education.

Finally, a woman who did much work for Catholic education in the late nineteenth century was St. Katharine Drexel; she dedicated herself to the education of Native Americans and blacks. She eventually founded the Sisters of the Blessed Sacrament for Indians and Colored People; they opened schools in Virginia and New Mexico, and most noted was their founding of a high school in New Orleans in 1915 that became Xavier University. By her death in 1955, the sisters had built sixty-two schools.

Teacher Training

As the number of Catholic schools increased, the numbers of both religious and lay teachers staffing the schools increased. Since in most cases the staff of these schools did not need to be state-certified, there were concerns about the methods used to prepare the teachers for formal classroom instruction. This situation led to examining methods of teacher training.

Newly ordained priests trained the teaching sisterhoods founded during America's colonial period. The trained sisters then shared what they learned with their communities: "With only a limited amount of time for the education of novices, congregations focused on character formation and general intellectual development; teacher training had a much lower priority. . . . It was the veteran sister-teachers who trained the novices in the ways of the Catholic classroom."[7]

Some orders wrote their own teacher handbooks. Sister of Notre Dame de Namur, Susan McGroarty (1827–1901), known as Sister Superior Julia, made training the sisters as teaching professionals her primary goal. "She began the practice of sending circular letters to sisters containing educational information and methodology. These letters were collected and published in the book called *Course of Studies*, a book that became the Sisters of Notre Dame de Namur system of education. It contained an outline of the curriculum for kindergarten through secondary education; much of it was written in German to accommodate the sisters in German parishes. The book was published in 1895 when Sister Julia was involved in the establishment of Trinity College in Washington, DC."[8]

In 1912, Burns wrote, "Some features of the Ursuline system of teaching were surprisingly modern, and throw a new light upon educational ideas and methods of the period. One of these features was the employment of pupil-teachers. They were selected from among the brightest and best-behaved girls, and their office was to assist the teachers in class work and in the maintenance of discipline. . . . The system was in many respects like the system of pupil teaching which was introduced almost a century later in the United States."[9]

During the first two-thirds of the nineteenth century, female religious often built schools with their own funds and operated them without any allegiance to a parish. Many European religious orders opened training centers in the United States to meet the need for parish schools, and new religious orders sprang up in the United States in response to this same need. One of the great advantages of these religious orders was that there was a single source for all the major components critical to the success of the school. The teachers were trained together so that they shared a common set of assumptions and goals. Since they took a vow of obedience to their superior in the order, they could be moved as needed throughout the network.

Mary Flavia Dunn (1856–1945), from the Sisters of the Holy Name, was known for the development of education in Oregon. She established a college at St. Mary's Academy in Portland in 1893, three normal schools for women, summer schools, and teacher institutes to help teachers achieve certification. The Felician Sisters (Sisters of St. Felix) established teacher-training programs and normal schools beginning in 1882. They later founded six colleges, including Felician College in Lodi, New Jersey.

Mary Molloy, a laywoman who eventually joined a Franciscan community, taught college courses for the Sisters of St. Francis in Minnesota, and she helped shape the College of St. Teresa into a prestigious liberal arts college in the early twentieth century. She developed a classical curriculum and challenged women to strive for greatness in both academics and public service.

The Twentieth Century

In 1900, only a handful of Catholic colleges for women were operating. The sisters whose founders taught in and governed Catholic colleges received the general training common to all sisters in postulant and novitiate programs. This situation improved during the first half of the twentieth century, and by 1968, there were approximately 170 colleges and seventy sister-formation colleges.[10] "Sister-teachers were prepared for the classroom by veteran teachers who were assigned as master to teachers. Teaching congregations also shared their success stories with one another."[11]

"As a result of trying to keep schools staffed, most nuns were sent out to teach directly after the novitiate, and then attended college during weekends and summers. This could take up to 20 years to earn a degree. In answer to the problem Rev. Thomas Shields opened a four-year sisters' college but some orders felt this would weaken the nuns' ties to their communities."[12]

The growth trend of Catholic schools called for more teachers than religious orders could provide. In the mid-1960s, about one-third of the teachers were lay teachers. By the fall of 1983, the proportion of lay teaching staff in elementary schools was almost four-fifths.

One must keep in mind that this change had an impact on the financial status of the schools. A nun's annual salary in Baltimore was only $200 in 1900, and this was paid to the order. Around this time, nuns still outnumbered priests by a ratio of four to one. Catholic education is still feeling the effects of the growing number of lay teachers needed to staff schools and of the salaries that these lay teachers need to live in the world.

Endnotes

1. Lawrence Lovasik (1990). *St. Joseph Church History: The Catholic Church through the Ages*. New York: Catholic Book Publishing Co., p. 133.

2. "Ladies of Charity of the USA: Vincentian Women." From www.famvin.org.

3. Timothy Walch (2003). *Parish School*. Washington, DC: NCEA, p. 20.

4. Mary Beth Celio (2004). "Lessons to Be Learned from Catholic Schools." From www.trinitydc.edu/newsevent/2004/snd/remarks/hayesm-php.

5. Glazier and Shelly, editors (1997). *Encyclopedia of American Catholic History*. Collegeville, MN: The Liturgical Press. Entries: Louise Van der Schrieck, p. 1260. Sisters of Notre Dame de Namur, pp. 1307-1309.

6. Glazier and Shelly, editors (1997). *Encyclopedia of American Catholic History*. Collegeville, MN: The Liturgical Press, pp. 1301–1307.

7. Timothy Walch (2003). *Parish School*. Washington, DC: NCEA, pp. 136–137.

8. Glazier and Shelly, editors (1997). *Encyclopedia of American Catholic History*. Collegeville, MN: The Liturgical Press, p. 886.

9. "Brother Aidan's Extracts 535." From http://archives.nd.edu/aidan/aidan535.htm.

10. Melanie Morey and John Piderit (2006). *Catholic Higher Education: A Culture in Crisis*. New York: Oxford University Press, pp. 246–247.

11. Mary Peter Travis (2000). "Preparation of Teachers," in *Catholic School Leadership*, edited by Hunt, Oldenski, and Wallace. New York: Falmer Press, pp. 142–143.

12. Melanie Morey and John Piderit (2006). *Catholic Higher Education: A Culture in Crisis*. New York: Oxford University Press, p. 248.

Other Sources

John Deedy (1984). "Beyond the Convent Wall: Sisters in the Modern World." *Theology Today*, Vol. 40, No. 4, January 1984.

John Fialka (2003). *Sisters: Catholic Nuns and the Making of America*. St. Martin's Press.

Catherine Kealey and Robert Kealey (2003). *On Their Shoulders: A Short Biographical History of American Catholic Schools*. Washington, DC: NCEA.

Charles Morris (1997). *American Catholic: The Saints and Sinners Who Built America's Most Powerful Church*. New York: Vintage.

Glazier and Shelly, editors (1997). *Encyclopedia of American Catholic History*. Collegeville, MN: The Liturgical Press.
Entries:
    Benedictines, pp. 136–146.
    Mary Frances Clarke, p. 351.
    Felician Sisters, pp. 504–505.
    Frances Xavier Cabrini, pp. 181–183.
    Marguerite Bourgeoys, pp. 952–953.
    Esther Parisea, p. 1110.
    Alice Lalor, pp. 1152–1155.
    Mary Elizabeth Lange, pp. 795–796.
    Ursulines, p. 1489.
    Cornelia Connelly, p. 372.
    Susan McGroarty, p. 886.
    Mary Flavia Dunn, pp. 467–468.
    Mary Molloy, p. 973.

Electronic Sources

"A Brief History of Vincentians." From www.vincentian.org.

"A Heritage of Loving Service: Sisters of St. Joseph of Carondelet in Tucson." From http://parentseyes.arizona.edu/carondelet/.

Sr. Mary Hayes. "Symposium Remarks." From www.trinity.edu.

www.ssnd.org

http://www.adriandominicans.org/WhoWeAre/AboutUs.aspx

"Life of St. Lucy Filippini." From http://www.filippiniusa.org/index.cfm?fuseaction=feature.display&feature_id=10.

www.spare.org

www.salesiansisters.org

"Religious of the Sacred Heart of Mary." From www.rshm.org/history.

CHAPTER 10

JUST PASSING THROUGH

Education

So in the end, how does one summarize the important beliefs about professional life that are fostered by twenty years of Catholic education? What do I remember about my education at Our Lady of the Miraculous Medal grammar school during the late 1950s and early 1960s?

Attending a parochial school meant going to Mass and confession while in school and being required to attend the Children's Mass on Sunday. It was the May Procession, the school fair, and the entire school walking to the neighborhood theater to see such movies as *Our Lady of Fatima*. For altar boys, it meant sometimes leaving school to serve at funeral Masses, serving the German Mass at eleven o'clock on Sundays, or helping the Sisters of Notre Dame de Namur out in the convent on Saturday mornings. The sisters exemplified the importance of high academic standards, Marian devotion, and living an overall Catholic life.

Unlike my parish grammar school, Christ the King High School served students from many different areas of Queens. Thanks to the Marist Brothers who staffed the school, the pressures of maintaining good grades were complemented by many athletic and social functions. School spirit, rivalry with a local Marist school, and loyalty to what we affectionately called CK were just part of the school culture of our late 1960s education. For those of us who had trouble mastering our studies, Saturdays meant help with Latin or math. The classes of forty to forty-five students didn't seem strange to us, and looking back I wonder how some of the teachers did it. Their struggles didn't discourage me; in fact, it was there that I was so intrigued by the example of the brothers and lay teachers that I firmly decided to become a teacher myself.

My undergraduate years were spent at St. John Fisher College in Rochester, New York. The campus was unabashedly imbued with Catholic culture owing to the presence of the Basilian Fathers who taught, monitored the dormitories, and administered the school. There were ample opportunities for service work in the inner city and in migrant worker communities on the outskirts of the city. I completed my internships and student teaching at local Catholic high schools.

This college experience, as well as my time living with other young men who shared my religious values, reinforced the ideals that I was taught in grammar and high school. They were not something that I left behind as I walked off the graduation line in 1965, 1969, 1976, or even 1999 with my doctoral hood from St. John's University. My religious, educational, and personal beliefs evolved as my personal and professional life did. As my goals changed, so did at least some of my ideals. The constant in my career has always been the belief that to teach is to serve with an emphasis on making a difference in the lives of others. As educators progress along their career paths, they find that they may make a difference in the lives of not only their students but also their colleagues, the teachers that they lead, or even the parents of the students that they serve. The mission of service expands.

Each of the four schools that I attended, including St. John's, began with the mission of serving youth in the community in which it began. Just as human beings change, so do institutions, and thus the missions of these schools were sometimes enlarged. These institutions were centered on the important beliefs of the orders that staffed them, and however different they were, their foundation was the work of the Church—that is, the work of Christ. What their teachers emphasized was influenced by the religious orders that ran them but also by American society of the time.

Teaching

My tenure as a math teacher in a Catholic high school was a rewarding one, in large part because I had the privilege of working with some of my former teachers. Saint Mary's Boys' High School was a suburban parish school staffed by the Marist Brothers. Owing to their example and that of dedicated lay colleagues, I learned a lot about caring for my students and setting high academic standards. Prayer, liturgy, and community service were integral parts of the school culture. I learned a great deal about being a principal from the two men who served in that office while I was there; this is somewhat ironic, though, because neither really wanted to be principal and both taught a class while holding the office. Their humility, cheerfulness, and concern for all in the building remind me to this day that one of the definitions of the Latin word *administrare* means "to help."

It did not take long for me to be deeply involved in the life of that school as I taught, coached, counseled, and even supervised student workers during the summer. It was a great way to begin a career in education, and for various reasons that experience renewed many of the ideals I had been taught as a student.

As a lay teacher myself, I took seriously the responsibility to care about my students and to be as generous with my time as possible. I was a product of the system of education offered by the brothers that I worked with, and thus it was easy for me to carry on the lessons I learned from them.

Nowadays, lay teachers need to reach out to those who may feel separated from or even abandoned by their Faith and educate them toward the Truth that is found in that Faith. This Truth is essential to understanding the meaning of life, the relationship that a person can have with God, and how these affect all other relationships that the student has. Faith also becomes a dimension of life, a lens through which everything is viewed and evaluated. This can be difficult for adolescents, who naturally question everything.

Teachers who are Catholic work in many public and non-Catholic private schools. While it may not be appropriate for them to openly discuss their religious viewpoints in non-Catholic schools, it is certainly their duty as Catholics to live their Faith in the workplace. Their actions and interactions with others should be based on their belief that God is within all of us. The truly Catholic teachers understand that their profession is actually a vocation, a calling not only to give of themselves wholeheartedly for the benefit of their students but also to become actively involved in the school community. Their interest in their students should continue outside of the classroom, and students should see them as adults who care about them, are interested in them, and are there for them when they need assistance and understanding. Benedictine hospitality and Salesian concern should be trademarks of their relationships with students, regardless of whether their pedagogy reflects the methods of Ignatius, de La Salle, or Bosco. It is not merely helpful but necessary to work with parents, especially when students encounter difficulty. This may call for helping parents to find the best sources of assistance for their son or daughter.

School Administration

Since those first seven years in education, I have worked as a teacher and administrator in several suburban public schools. My desire to seek out what is needed and attempt to help fill that need was a lesson from my own teachers and the teachers and administrators who became my colleagues. Twice in my career their example led me, though perhaps in a circuitous fashion, through a myriad of supervisory and administrative positions to a principal's office.

At the end of my first year as a principal, I authored an article about my experience. I concluded those thoughts with the following statements:

> The principal's position is rewarding, challenging and enjoyable. To survive criticism or appreciate praise, the principal must be grounded in ideals and values. He must be an articulate cheerleader, who expresses gratitude for jobs well done, and a challenger of staff who know that he/she believes in them. When students or parents come to him in their lowest moments and they ask the unanswerable questions such as "Why me?" or "What do we do with our son/daughter?" the principal must only respond with sincere sympathy. He can become a parent away from home or a confidant to adolescents who experience anything ranging from tragic situations such as abuse or loss of a parent to more typical adolescent problems. This part of my professional career has always been very meaningful and rewarding. The principal must create a supportive climate for staff, yet constantly raise the bar for their performance. He must model the willingness to take responsibility when a job is not well done. Disappointment, fatigue, and impatience must be in service to a smile for all who pass him. He must be a constant reminder to

all that we are here to serve students and their families.[1]

When Catholic educators are also administrators, they should maintain relationships with those they supervise, in much the same way that teachers interact with their students. The literature on Catholic leadership is rich, and regardless of whether it is written from the point of view of an abbot, a superior of a religious order, or a principal, the common theme is leadership as service. There are constant reminders of a leader's responsibility for the development and wellbeing of those who are subordinate to him or her. Correction is to be given with love and as a path of personal development for the person being disciplined. Decisions are made for the good of the whole, following collaboration and sometimes prayer. Decision making is centered on the mission of the school.

The administrator should lead the community in the manner of the Benedictine abbot. Kindness and understanding should be the trademarks of the professional relationship that holds all accountable for their work with students. The school leader must have patience with the nervous new teacher as well as the uncooperative veteran teachers. He or she must hold high standards for students and teachers, always serving as a model for the traits that he or she wishes to be seen by all in the school community.

Much of what I have learned along the way came not only from the adults who influenced me during my youth and the colleagues with whom I shared my professional journey but also from the students with whom I worked.

If we motivate our students to achieve success, their success is, in part, ours. In the course of a day, a smile, a brief conversation, or a question as to how one is doing can have a significant impact on a student, even when we don't realize it. If we touch the hearts of a few students by letting them express their feelings and concerns to us, they gain confidence in their relationship with us and may turn to us when they need help. The reward is that there are a few times when you know that you have been an instrument of the Holy Spirit, times when you do not know the source of the words that you spoke in your attempts to comfort or offer advice. This may not happen often, but the results of your efforts may still surprise you.

There have been times when public school students broached the subject of God during a conversation with me. Some have found it difficult to believe in God, given their difficult circumstances; others have said that He is an important presence in their lives. In that case I try to reinforce the importance of religion in their lives, regardless of the faith they practice, and to emphasize the important dimension that it adds to their lives. Some have told me that they took great comfort in stopping by a church or attending services. This could have been their calm in the midst of their storms. I have been pleasantly surprised at the honest thoughts and feelings that some have shared with me on this topic, and I try to remember these moments when I am discouraged by what seems to be the futility of my efforts.

As was previously stated, I believe that to be an administrator is to minister to your school community. This means proactively searching for those who need help and realizing that those who need assistance the most are often most reluctant to ask for it. It may mean taking the time to look at report cards and following up with students who are having some academic difficulties or are frequently absent. Many times there are causes for these "red flags" that would go unnoticed if nobody cared enough to ask. Teens do not usually ask for help. Boys especially are embarrassed to talk about problems at home or those that they face individually. When parents are experiencing marital problems, financial difficulties, or the sickness of a loved one, they may tell their sons and daughters to not talk about it. If an older sibling has mental health problems or is abusing drugs or alcohol, families do not want anyone to know. Often students feel that they are betraying their family by talking to someone. Then again, students themselves may feel betrayed.

When students are absent because of a death in the family, it is important to follow up with them when they return. Youth have a terrible time dealing with death. The death of a grandparent is often their introduction to this part of life. Those from close families need comfort. Sometimes they need a place to cry or express their feelings away from their families.

We also should remember that adolescence can be a difficult period even when there are no serious problems to contend with. Our most successful and active students can become overwhelmed; they may need someone to listen to them if they work too hard or experience excessive pressure from themselves or their parents. And there are certain times of the year when students get stressed out: seniors get mentally exhausted during the college application process, and many students experience anxiety at the middle and the end of the semester when exams and projects pile up. In addition, when students participate in sports or clubs that take a lot of their time, they may need encouragement when they do not achieve the success they desire. It is important for administrators to attend games, performances, and other activities to demonstrate their support. It also means a lot to students if you take a moment to congratulate them for a special achievement or to compliment them for hanging in there through a difficult situation. Our young men and women need to be appreciated; sometimes their parents take them for granted, and they need to be reminded of how special they are for all that they do.

The Catholic Lens

School politics, changes in family structure, drug and alcohol abuse, and declining values in schools can make educators' challenges seem insurmountable and their accomplishments superficial. It is ironic that as I read the literature regarding problems in public schools, including bullying, violence, and prejudice, the proposed solutions—such as the need for character and ethics education and the importance of creating a school community—can all be found in the history and philosophy of Catholic education. John Bosco's preventive method of teacher presence and vigilance is often cited as important in preventing bullying. Establishing community means identifying the values for a school and emphasizing its unique history and traditions. Instruction in values and morality certainly is one of the purposes for which Catholic schools exist, and this could be carried over to the public sector in a nonsectarian manner.

While some of what I have suggested may seem rather idealistic, I would hope that each of us can remember some of our own teachers and school administrators who exemplified such traits and carried out their responsibilities in these ways. I believe that the way that they performed their duties was related to their spiritual lives.

When I was a student, many of the priests, sisters, and brothers who taught us lived the flow of the Church year by reading the breviary. The liturgical calendar, including the saints' feast days, formed the basis of their prayer and spiritual reading each day. At the end of a few years, they had read all of the Scriptures that the Church has deemed most important as well as some writings of the doctors of the Church and other saints. These readings gave a rhythm to their lives, a rhythm which to some degree they passed on to their parishioners and students. This is also part of what makes Catholic life unique. In some sense, our lives would have less meaning without the Church year, which makes what seems like any normal day truly different from the next.

It would be worthwhile for the Catholic teacher to follow, for two or three years, the daily readings of the Church. It not only "consecrates" each day but also can become a source of motivation and inspiration. The readings of the Church offer us the beauty and inspiration of Scripture and also pass on the lessons that the saints teach us. We can use their lives as models to admire and to imitate.

Fortunately for us weaker souls, not all saints tortured themselves with frightening penances, died as martyrs, or utterly separated themselves from the world. There are many saints with whom we can identify because they shared the work that fills our lives: serving others in schools. Some of these saints have schools, churches, orphanages, and hospitals named after them. Others are the very people who first brought our religion to this country. While many missionaries were not classroom teachers in the typical sense, who would deny that they who taught the Faith to and started schools for Native Americans in the western and southern missions were true teachers? Their names—such as Marquette, Le Moyne, and Junípero Serra—are also names of colleges.

Their professional lives were not easy. Many of those who went before us faced challenges and false accusations, yet they successfully lived out their vocation. Their lives were not all that different from ours. The examples are many.

Holy Cross founder Bails Moreau died without contact from the brothers and priests of the order he founded. Saint John Baptist de La Salle was criticized for catering to the poor and not concentrating on the more privileged. Saint John Bosco was thought crazy by some, and other founders were criticized by the religious that they led. Pettiness, jealousy, and misunderstanding are common in all states of life and, unfortunately, in all communities. It takes an understanding of human nature and a developed interior life, to not give up. We are fortunate to have a legacy of many individuals who exhibited these qualities, and I believe that we would be rather remiss if we did not take the time to garner some lessons from their experiences.

Every once in a while, I come across an article that has a deep meaning for me at a particular time. I will quote from two; I believe that these authors can remind us all of something important. The first is entitled "The Call to Teach: Spirituality and Intellectual Life," by Lillie Albert of Boston College: "When I linked my spiritual and my intellectual life and grounded them both in my work as a mathematics educator, I was more substantially living out the message of the mission of the Jesuit University."[2]

In the second, entitled "Spirituality and the Academic Vocation," Richard Liddy asks how we can recover that initial inspiration for our teaching vocation, despite the power politics and turf wars, many of us face.[3] His answer is that spirituality is a way in which we can rediscover that passion.

The underlying theme in both of these articles is that viewing our career through a spiritual lens gives our lives greater meaning, bestows strength amidst difficulty, and renews our commitment.

The development of the spiritual life begins in the home and the lower schools. The lessons of the Sisters of Notre Dame de Namur and the Marist Brothers have grown with me. While faith and prayer life were stressed, so were service to others and scholarship. A love for learning, reading, and some quiet time to reflect remains with me to this day. Because of my background, I readily follow my inclination to return to a quiet church and find peace in the flicker of the sanctuary candle. This place of refuge reminds me that there is a Presence much greater than I can imagine, a Presence that profoundly affects my journey in life. I am thankful for that Presence that I believe was somehow with me during my career, and I am excited by the question of where it will lead me during retirement.

Endnotes

1. Wayne Merckling (2001). "Personal Reflections of a First-Year Principal." *Educational Viewpoints*, Vol. 21, No. 1, pp. 17–19.

2. Lillie Albert (2000). "The Call to Teach: Spirituality and Intellectual Life." *Conversations*, Vol. 18, Fall, pp. 38–42.

3. Richard Liddy (2000). "Spirituality and the Academic Vocation" from the proceedings of the Center for Catholic Studies. "I Have Called You by Name: Spirituality and the Academic Vocation," Summer Seminar 2000, Seton Hall University, South Orange, New Jersey.

Other Sources

Craig Galbraith and Oliver Galbraith (2004). *The Benedictine Rule of Leadership*. Massachusetts: Adams Media.

Chris Lowney (2003). *Heroic Leadership*. Maryland: Loyola Press.

About the Author

Wayne Merckling, EdD, completed his BA in Mathematics at St. John Fisher College, Rochester, New York, and his MS in Mathematics Education and EdD in School Leadership at St. John's University in Queens, New York. Wayne served for over forty years as a secondary teacher and administrator in Nassau County, New York, as well as in Morris and Bergen Counties, New Jersey.

About Leonine Publishers

Leonine Publishers LLC makes fine Catholic literature available to Catholics throughout the English-speaking world. Leonine Publishers offers an innovative "hybrid" approach to book publication that helps authors as well as readers. Please visit our web site at www.leoninepublishers.com to learn more about us. Browse our online bookstore to find more solid Catholic titles to uplift, challenge, and inspire.

Our patron and namesake is Pope Leo XIII, a prudent, yet uncompromising pope during the stormy years at the close of the 19th century. Please join us as we ask his intercession for our family of readers and authors.

Do you have a book inside you? Visit our web site today. Leonine Publishers accepts manuscripts from Catholic authors like you. If your book is selected for publication, you will have an active part in the production process. This book is an example of our growing selection of literature for the busy Catholic reader of the 21st century.

www.leoninepublishers.com

CPSIA information can be obtained
at www.ICGtesting.com
Printed in the USA
FFOW04n1443260115
10520FF

9 781942 190080